ISEE Lower Level Math workbook

Math Exercises, Activities, and Two Full-Length ISEE Lower Level Math Practice Tests

By

Michael Smith & Reza Nazari

ISEE Lower Level Math Workbook

WWW.MathNotion.COM

… So Much More Online!

✓ FREE Math Lessons

✓ More Math Learning Books!

✓ Mathematics Worksheets

✓ Online Math Tutors

For a PDF Version of This Book

Please Visit WWW.MathNotion.com

ISEE Lower Level Math Workbook
Published in the United State of America By
The Math Notion
Email: info@Mathnotion.com
Web: www.MathNotion.com

About the Author

Michael Smith has been a math instructor for over a decade now. He holds a master's degree in Management. Since 2006, Michael has devoted his time to both teaching and developing exceptional math learning materials. As a Math instructor and test prep expert, Michael has worked with thousands of students. He has used the feedback of his students to develop a unique study program that can be used by students to drastically improve their math score fast and effectively.

   – **SAT Math Workbook**

   – **PSAT Math Workbook**

   – **ACT Math Workbook**

   – **GRE Math Workbook**

   – **SSAT Math Workbooks**

   – **Common Core Math Workbooks**

   –**many Math Education Workbooks**

   – **and some Mathematics books …**

As an experienced Math teacher, Mr. Smith employs a variety of formats to help students achieve their goals: He tutors online and in person, he teaches students in large groups, and he provides training materials and textbooks through his website and through Amazon.

You can contact Michael via email at:

   info@Mathnotion.com

ISEE Lower Level Math Workbook

ISEE Lower Level Math Workbook reviews all ISEE Lower Level and provides students with the confidence and math skills they need the ISEE Lower Level Math. It is designed to address the needs of IS Level test takers who must have a working knowledge of basic Math This comprehensive workbook with over 2,500 sample questions and ISEE Lower Level tests can help you fully prepare for the ISEE Low test. It provides you with an in-depth focus on the math portion of th helping you master the math skills that students find the most troubl an incredibly useful tool for those who want to review all topics bei the ISEE Lower Level Math test.

ISEE Lower Level Math Workbook contains many exciting featu prepare for the ISEE Lower Level Math test, including:

- Content 100% aligned with the 2019-2020 ISEE Lower Level
- Provided and tested by ISEE Lower Level Math test experts
- Dynamic design and easy-to-follow activities
- A fun, interactive and concrete learning process
- Targeted, skill-building practices
- Complete coverage of all ISEE Lower Level Math topics wh tested
- 2 full-length practice tests (featuring new question types) wit answers.

The only prep book you will ever need to ace the ISEE Low Test!

Contents

Chapter 1: Place Values and Number Sense

Topics that you'll learn in this chapter:

- ✓ Place Values

- ✓ Compare Numbers

- ✓ Numbers in Word

- ✓ Roman Numerals

- ✓ Rounding

- ✓ Odd or Even

- ✓ Pattern

- ✓ Growing Pattern

Place Values

✎ Write numbers in expanded form.

1) Seventy–one   ___ + ___

2) eighty–five   ___ + ___

3) twenty–three   ___ + ___

4) fifty–four   ___ + ___

5) Ninety–nine   ___ + ___

✎ Circle the correct choice.

6) The 4 in 94 is in the

                 Ones place   tens place   hundreds place

7) The 8 in 84 is in the

                 Ones place   tens place   hundreds place

8) The 6 in 672 is in the

                 Ones place   tens place   hundreds place

9) The 2 in 921 is in the

                 Ones place   tens place   hundreds place

10) The 7 in 157 is in the

                 Ones place   tens place   hundreds place

Comparing and Ordering Numbers

✍ Use less than, equal to or greater than.

1) 42 _____ 46

2) 89 _____ 79

3) 59 _____ 55

4) 96 _____ 92

5) 89 _____ 89

6) 69 _____ 63

7) 99 _____ 89

8) 38 _____ 25

9) 44 _____ 44

10) 89 _____ 98

11) 16 _____ 26

12) 79 _____ 68

13) 48 _____ 55

14) 13 _____ 31

✍ Order each set numbers from least to greatest.

15) – 15, – 19, 25, – 16, 1   ___, ___, ___, ___, ___, ___

16) 18, –26, 8, – 9, 3   ___, ___, ___, ___, ___, ___

17) 26, – 46, 30, 0, – 26   ___, ___, ___, ___, ___, ___

18) 16, – 86, 0, – 16, 77, –65   ___, ___, ___, ___, ___, ___

19) –20, –81, 80, –36, –69, –49   ___, ___, ___, ___, ___, ___

20) 99, 15, 49, 18, 89, 20   ___, ___, ___, ___, ___, ___

21) 89, 19, 29, 18, 39, 27   ___, ___, ___, ___, ___, ___

Write Numbers in Words

✍ Write each number in words.

1) 456 _____

2) 907 _____

3) 740 _____

4) 132 _____

5) 535 _____

6) 831 _____

7) 2,117 _____

8) 1,578 _____

9) 4,521 _____

10) 5,787 _____

11) 6,672 _____

12) 8,490 _____

13) 3,247 _____

14) 9,019 _____

15) 10,561 _____

Roman Numerals

✍ Write in Romans numerals.

1	I	11	XI	21	XXI
2	II	12	XII	22	XXII
3	III	13	XIII	23	XXIII
4	IV	14	XIV	24	XXIV
5	V	15	XV	25	XXV
6	VI	16	XVI	26	XXVI
7	VII	17	XVII	27	XXVII
8	VIII	18	XVIII	28	XXVIII
9	IX	19	XIX	29	XXIX
10	X	20	XX	30	XXX

1) 13 _____

2) 26 _____

3) 23 _____

4) 19 _____

5) 25 _____

6) 1 8 _____

7) 1 4 _____

8) 9 _____

9) 17 _____

10) 34 _____

11) Add 8 + 13 and write in Roman numerals. _____

12) Subtract 22 – 9 and write in Roman numerals. _____

Rounding Numbers

✍ Round each number to the underlined place value.

1) 2,<u>8</u>82

2) 4,<u>9</u>85

3) 45<u>6</u>3

4) 4,2<u>8</u>1

5) 9,3<u>5</u>6

6) 2,3<u>6</u>4

7) 6,<u>2</u>09

8) 1,3<u>5</u>6

9) 7,<u>3</u>71

10) 8,9<u>2</u>3

11) 5,5<u>4</u>9

12) <u>8</u>,246

13) 10,4<u>6</u>2

14) 2,<u>6</u>98

15) 1,<u>2</u>50

16) 7,<u>6</u>45

17) 9,4<u>9</u>6

18) 5,4<u>3</u>9

19) 8,5<u>9</u>3

20) 11,<u>9</u>39

21) 1<u>9</u>,802

22) 15,4<u>5</u>5

23) 26,<u>8</u>45

24) 9,7<u>1</u>9

Odd or Even

✍ Identify whether each number is even or odd.

1) 28 _____

2) 23 _____

3) 25 _____

4) 15 _____

5) 55 _____

6) 88 _____

7) 42 _____

8) 97 _____

9) 72 _____

10) 60 _____

11) 33 _____

12) 101 _____

✍ Circle the even number in each group.

13) 12, 21, 47, 63, 9, 53

14) 19, 17, 107, 43, 35, 48

15) 29, 37, 64, 57, 65, 99

16) 77, 18, 89, 67, 27, 83

✍ Circle the odd number in each group.

17) 42, 24, 22, 64, 93, 98

18) 18, 26, 20, 44, 66, 75

19) 48, 82, 13, 98, 64, 56

20) 97, 52, 58, 46, 38, 102

Repeating Pattern

✍ Circle the picture that comes next in each picture pattern.

1) ◇ ▲ ◇ ▲ ◇   ▲ ◇

2) ◇ ⬠ ⬠ ◇ ⬠   ⬠ ◇

3) ⬭ ✶ ⬭ ✶ ⬭   ⬭ ✶

4) ♥ ♥ ☺ ☺ ♥   ♥ ☺

5) ⬭ ✶ ♥ ⬭ ✶   ♥ ✶

Growing Patterns

✎ Draw the picture that comes next in each growing pattern.

1)

2)

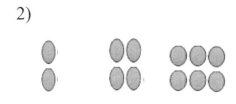

3)

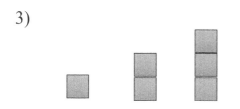

4)

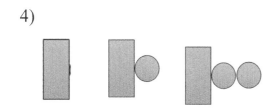

5)

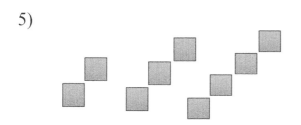

Patterns: Numbers

✍ Write the numbers that come next.

1) 3, 6, 9, 12,   _____, _____, _____, _____

2) 5, 10, 15, 20,   _____, _____, _____, _____

3) 2, 6, 10, 14,   _____, _____, _____, _____

4) 12, 22, 32, 42,   _____, _____, _____, _____

5) 7, 14, 21, 28,   _____, _____, _____, _____

6) 10, 18, 26, 34, 42,   _____, _____, _____, _____

✍ Write the next three numbers in each counting sequence.

1) –41, –29, –17, _____, _____, _____, _____

2) 652, 637, 622, _____, _____, _____, _____

3) 15, 25, _____, _____, 55, _____

4) 25, 33, _____, _____, _____

5) 77, 66, _____, _____, _____

6) 82, 69, 56, _____, _____, _____

7) 256, 224, 192, _____, _____, _____

8) What are the next three numbers in this counting sequence?

   2350, 2450, 2550, _____, _____, _____

9) What is the sixth number in this counting sequence?

   7, 15, 23, _____

Answers of Worksheets – Chapter 1

Place Values

1) 70 + 1

2) 80 + 5

3) 20 + 3

4) 50 + 4

5) 90 + 9

6) ones place

7) tens place

8) hundreds place

9) tens place

10) one place

Comparing and Ordering Numbers

1) 42 less than 46

2) 89greater than 79

3) 59 greater than 55

4) 96 greater than 92

5) 89 equals to 89

6) 69 greater than 63

7) 99 greater than 89

8) 38 greater than 25

9) 44 equals to 44

10) 89 less than 98

11) 16 less than 26

12) 79 greater than 68

13) 48 less than 55

14) 13 less than 31

15) –19, –16, –15, 1, 25

16) –26, –9, 3, 8, 18

17) –46, –26, 0, 26, 30

18) –86, –65, –16, 0, 16, 77

19) –81, –69, –49, –35, –20, 80

20) 15, 18, 20,49, 89, 99

21) 18, 19, 27,29, 39, 89

Word Names for Numbers

1) four hundred fifty-six

2) nine hundred seven

3) seven hundred forty

4) one hundred thirty-two

5) five hundred thirty -five

6) eight hundred thirty- one

7) two thousand, one hundred seventeen

8) one thousand, five hundred seventy-eight

9) four thousand, five hundred twenty-one

10) five thousand, seven hundred eighty-seven

11) sex thousand, six hundred seventy-two

12) eight thousand, four hundred ninety

13) three thousand, two hundred forty-seven

14) nine thousand, nineteen

15) ten thousand, five hundred sixty-one

Roman Numerals

1) XIII

2) XXVI

3) XXIII

4) XIX

5) XXV

6) XVIII

7) XIV

8) IX

9) XVII

10) XXXIV

11) XXI

12) XIII

Rounding Numbers

1) 2,900

2) 5,000

3) 4,560

4) 4,280

5) 9,360

6) 2,360

7) 6,200

8) 1,360

9) 7,400

10) 8,920

11) 5,550

12) 8,000

13) 10,460	16) 7,600	19) 8,590	22) 15,460
14) 2,700	17) 9,500	20) 11,900	23) 26,800
15) 1,300	18) 5,440	21) 20,000	24) 9,720

Odd or Even

1) even	6) even	11) odd	16) 18
2) odd	7) even	12) odd	17) 93
3) odd	8) odd	13) 12	18) 75
4) odd	9) even	14) 48	19) 13
5) odd	10) even	15) 64	20) 97

Repeating pattern

1)   2)   3)

4) 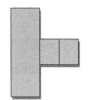   5)

Growing patterns

1) 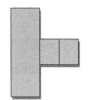   2)    3)

4)    5)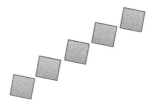

Patterns: Numbers

1) 3, 6, 9, 12, 15, 18, 21, 24

2) 5, 10, 15, 20, 25, 30, 35, 40

3) 2, 6, 10, 14, 18, 22, 26, 30

4) 12, 22, 32, 42, 52, 62, 72, 82

5) 7, 14, 21, 28, 35, 42, 49, 56

6) 10, 18, 26, 34, 42, 50, 58, 66

Patterns

1) –5, 7, 19, 31

2) 607, 592, 577, 562

3) 15–25–35–45–55–65

4) 41–49–57

5) 55–44–33

6) 43, 30, 17

7) 160, 128, 96

8) 2650–2750–2850

9) 31

Chapter 2: Whole Number Operations

Topics that you'll learn in this chapter:

- ✓ Adding Whole Numbers

- ✓ Subtracting Whole Numbers

- ✓ Multiplying Whole Numbers

- ✓ Dividing Hundreds

- ✓ Long Division by One Digit

- ✓ Division with Remainders

- ✓ Rounding Whole Numbers

- ✓ Whole Number Estimation

Adding Whole Numbers

✍ Add.

1)
$$\begin{array}{r} 4{,}456 \\ +\ 7{,}987 \\ \hline \\ \hline \end{array}$$

4)
$$\begin{array}{r} 4{,}379 \\ +9{,}480 \\ \hline \\ \hline \end{array}$$

2)
$$\begin{array}{r} 5{,}376 \\ +\ 2{,}588 \\ \hline \\ \hline \end{array}$$

5)
$$\begin{array}{r} 7{,}768 \\ +4{,}384 \\ \hline \\ \hline \end{array}$$

3)
$$\begin{array}{r} 4{,}699 \\ +\ 2{,}552 \\ \hline \\ \hline \end{array}$$

6)
$$\begin{array}{r} 6{,}069 \\ +\ 2{,}099 \\ \hline \\ \hline \end{array}$$

✍ Find the missing numbers.

7) $2{,}265 + \underline{\quad} = 2{,}365$

10) $608 + \underline{\quad} = 1{,}998$

8) $650 + 1{,}200 = \underline{\quad}$

11) $\underline{\quad} + 551 = 4{,}561$

9) $2{,}500 + \underline{\quad} = 6{,}900$

12) $\underline{\quad} + 1{,}890 = 3{,}951$

13) David sells gems. He finds a diamond in Istanbul and buys it for $3,879. Then, he flies to Cairo and purchases a bigger diamond for the bargain price of $8,156. How much does David spend on the two diamonds?

Subtracting Whole Numbers

✏Subtract.

1)
$$\begin{array}{r} 8,639 \\ -7,162 \\ \hline \end{array}$$

4)
$$\begin{array}{r} 7,056 \\ -4,009 \\ \hline \end{array}$$

2)
$$\begin{array}{r} 4,267 \\ -1,448 \\ \hline \end{array}$$

5)
$$\begin{array}{r} 9,115 \\ -7,956 \\ \hline \end{array}$$

3)
$$\begin{array}{r} 7,651 \\ -4,913 \\ \hline \end{array}$$

6)
$$\begin{array}{r} 3,001 \\ -1,869 \\ \hline \end{array}$$

✏Find the missing number.

7) $4,560 - \underline{\quad} = 2,582$

10) $3,400 - \underline{\quad} = 1,698$

8) $8,512 - \underline{\quad} = 3,569$

11) $8,642 - 6,987 = \underline{\quad}$

9) $7,243 - 1,875 = \underline{\quad}$

12) $7,410 - 4,568 = \underline{\quad}$

13) Jackson had \$5,437 invested in the stock market until he lost \$3,891 on those investments. How much money does he have in the stock market now?

_____

Multiplying Whole Numbers

✎Find the answers.

1)
$$\begin{array}{r} 1100 \\ \times\ 22 \\ \hline \end{array}$$

2)
$$\begin{array}{r} 4100 \\ \times\ 15 \\ \hline \end{array}$$

3)
$$\begin{array}{r} 7960 \\ \times\ 2 \\ \hline \end{array}$$

4)
$$\begin{array}{r} 6000 \\ \times\ 4 \\ \hline \end{array}$$

5)
$$\begin{array}{r} 4500 \\ \times\ 2 \\ \hline \end{array}$$

6)
$$\begin{array}{r} 1400 \\ \times 20 \\ \hline \end{array}$$

7)
$$\begin{array}{r} 3129 \\ \times 24 \\ \hline \end{array}$$

8)
$$\begin{array}{r} 9510 \\ \times\ 23 \\ \hline \end{array}$$

9)
$$\begin{array}{r} 3213 \\ \times\ 65 \\ \hline \end{array}$$

10)
$$\begin{array}{r} 5400 \\ \times\ 17 \\ \hline \end{array}$$

11)
$$\begin{array}{r} 3700 \\ \times\ 11 \\ \hline \end{array}$$

12)
$$\begin{array}{r} 9000 \\ \times\ 33 \\ \hline \end{array}$$

Dividing Hundreds

✍ Find answers.

1) 2000 ÷ 200

2) 1600 ÷ 20

3) 900 ÷ 100

4) 3,200 ÷ 800

5) 4,800 ÷ 800

6) 900 ÷ 300

7) 2,400 ÷ 800

8) 4,500 ÷ 900

9) 6,800 ÷ 200

10) 10,000 ÷ 200

11) 8,100 ÷ 300

12) 8,000 ÷ 500

13) 1,200 ÷ 200

14) 6,600 ÷ 600

15) 7,200 ÷ 600

16) 1,800 ÷ 200

17) 27,000 ÷ 900

18) 9,900 ÷ 300

19) 7,200 ÷ 100

20) 9,000 ÷ 120

21) 9,000 ÷ 3,000

22) 16,000 ÷ 40

23) 210 ÷ 30

24) 560 ÷ 70

Long Division by Two Digit

✍ Find the quotient.

1) $16\overline{)512}$

2) $12\overline{)816}$

3) $24\overline{)672}$

4) $28\overline{)364}$

5) $34\overline{)578}$

6) $36\overline{)324}$

7) $21\overline{)651}$

8) $42\overline{)2,142}$

9) $65\overline{)1,300}$

10) $45\overline{)1,620}$

11) $63\overline{)2,961}$

12) $50\overline{)2,400}$

13) $27\overline{)2,457}$

14) $67\overline{)7,303}$

15) $93\overline{)4,092}$

16) $76\overline{)6,156}$

17) $70\overline{)12,880}$

18) $18\overline{)11,088}$

Division with Remainders

✍ Find the quotient with remainder.

1) $12\overline{)613}$

2) $15\overline{)2,579}$

3) $23\overline{)3,923}$

4) $81\overline{)3,566}$

5) $38\overline{)6,996}$

6) $75\overline{)8,009}$

7) $59\overline{)7,512}$

8) $85\overline{)11,264}$

9) $45\overline{)7,335}$

10) $88\overline{)12,589}$

11) $36\overline{)9,564}$

12) $60\overline{)36,947}$

13) $78\overline{)6,298}$

14) $95\overline{)37,456}$

Rounding Whole Numbers

✎ Round each number to the underlined place value.

1) 5,9<u>4</u>4

2) 7,<u>5</u>64

3) 7,7<u>7</u>4

4) 3,4<u>8</u>6

5) 6,6<u>7</u>5

6) 1,1<u>5</u>4

7) 4,<u>6</u>04

8) 10,5<u>5</u>9

9) 9,<u>4</u>74

10) 2,8<u>1</u>5

11) 3,9<u>4</u>8

12) 10,<u>2</u>49

13) 4,<u>5</u>63

14) 9,6<u>8</u>5

15) 4,4<u>3</u>0

16) 1,<u>6</u>86

17) 3,<u>6</u>50

18) 14,<u>0</u>50

19) <u>7</u>,222

20) 2,5<u>3</u>5

21) 11,<u>9</u>65

22) 15,4<u>5</u>5

23) 26,0<u>2</u>5

24) 27,5<u>7</u>9

25) 6,<u>4</u>01

26) 4,1<u>2</u>3

27) 2,<u>8</u>95

Whole Number Estimation

✎Estimate the sum by rounding each added to the nearest ten.

1) 965 + 485

2) 1,956 + 2,745

3) 5,424 + 3,562

4) 2,743 + 8,246

5) 2,585 + 5,682

6) 5,754 + 8,386

7) 4,528 + 5,324

8) 8,755 + 3,155

9)
$$\begin{array}{r} 2,864 \\ + 9,547 \\ \hline \end{array}$$

10)
$$\begin{array}{r} 7,531 \\ + 8,765 \\ \hline \end{array}$$

11)
$$\begin{array}{r} 7,523 \\ + 2,388 \\ \hline \end{array}$$

12)
$$\begin{array}{r} 5,379 \\ + 7,445 \\ \hline \end{array}$$

13)
$$\begin{array}{r} 3,168 \\ + 5,025 \\ \hline \end{array}$$

14)
$$\begin{array}{r} 2,270 \\ + 4,129 \\ \hline \end{array}$$

Answers of Worksheets – Chapter 2

Adding Whole Numbers

1) 12,443	6) 8,168	11) 4,010
2) 7,964	7) 100	12) 2,061
3) 7,251	8) 1,850	13) $12,035
4) 13,859	9) 4,400	
5) 12,152	10) 13,90	

Subtracting Whole Numbers

1) 1,477	6) 1,132	11) 1,655
2) 2,819	7) 1,978	12) 2,842
3) 2,738	8) 4,943	13) 1,546
4) 3,047	9) 5,368	
5) 1,159	10) 1,702	

Multiplying Whole Numbers

1) 24,200	5) 9,000	9) 208,845
2) 61,500	6) 28,000	10) 91,800
3) 15,920	7) 75,096	11) 40,700
4) 24,000	8) 218,730	12) 297,000

Dividing Whole Numbers

1) 10	7) 3	13) 6	19) 75
2) 80	8) 5	14) 11	20) 75
3) 9	9) 34	15) 12	21) 3
4) 4	10) 50	16) 9	22) 400
5) 6	11) 27	17) 30	23) 7
6) 3	12) 16	18) 33	24) 8

Long Division by One Digit

1) 32	5) 17	9) 20	13) 91
2) 68	6) 9	10) 36	14) 109
3) 28	7) 31	11) 47	15) 44
4) 13	8) 51	12) 48	16) 81

17) 184   18) 616

Division with Remainders

1) 51 R1   6) 106 R59   11) 265 R24

2) 171 R14   7) 127 R19   12) 615 R47

3) 170 R13   8) 132 R44   13) 80 R58

4) 44 R2   9) 163 R0   14) 394 R26

5) 184 R4   10) 143 R5

Rounding Whole Numbers

1) 5,900   10) 2,820   19) 7,000

2) 7,600   11) 3,950   20) 2,540

3) 7,770   12) 10,200   21) 12,000

4) 3,490   13) 5,000   22) 15460

5) 6,680   14) 9,690   23) 26030

6) 1,150   15) 4,400   24) 27,580

7) 4,600   16) 1,700   25) 6,400

8) 10,560   17) 3,700   26) 4,120

9) 9,500   18) 14,100   27) 2,900

Whole Number Estimation

1) 1,460   6) 14,140   11) 9,910

2) 4,710   7) 9,850   12) 12,830

3) 8,980   8) 11,920   13) 8,200

4) 10,990   9) 12,410   14) 6,400

5) 8,270   10) 16,300

Chapter 3: Number Theory

Topics that you'll learn in this chapter:

- ✓ Factoring Numbers

- ✓ Prime Factorization

- ✓ Divisibility Rules

- ✓ Greatest Common Factor

- ✓ Least Common Multiple

Factoring Numbers

✍List all positive factors of each number.

1) 14	6) 75	11) 39
2) 18	7) 66	12) 35
3) 32	8) 60	13) 54
4) 42	9) 38	14) 22
5) 24	10) 52	15) 84

✍List the prime factorization for each number.

16) 12	19) 45	22) 49
17) 36	20) 50	23) 85
18) 22	21) 64	24) 94

Prime Factorization

✍Factor the following numbers to their prime factors.

1) 15	9) 66	17) 91
2) 22	10) 36	18) 30
3) 9	11) 14	19) 8
4) 24	12) 56	20) 12
5) 16	13) 52	21) 63
6) 34	14) 70	22) 33
7) 28	15) 84	23) 35
8) 26	16) 22	24) 54

Divisibility Rules

✍ Use the divisibility rules to underline the factors of the number.

1) 10   2 3 4 5 6 7 8 9 10

2) 12   2 3 4 5 6 7 8 9 10

3) 24   2 3 4 5 6 7 8 9 10

4) 15   2 3 4 5 6 7 8 9 10

5) 30   2 3 4 5 6 7 8 9 10

6) 5   2 3 4 5 6 7 8 9 10

7) 32   2 3 4 5 6 7 8 9 10

8) 48   2 3 4 5 6 7 8 9 10

9) 16   2 3 4 5 6 7 8 9 10

10) 25   2 3 4 5 6 7 8 9 10

11) 35   2 3 4 5 6 7 8 9 10

12) 49   2 3 4 5 6 7 8 9 10

Greatest Common Factor

✎ Find the GCF for each number pair.

1) 20, 30	9) 32, 4	17) 65, 49
2) 6, 14	10) 17, 21	18) 50, 45
3) 5, 35	11) 16, 2	19) 98, 10
4) 48, 12	12) 49, 7	20) 50, 25
5) 17, 13	13) 32, 36	21) 110, 40
6) 33, 27	14) 80, 70	22) 36, 12
7) 12, 15	15) 82, 42	23) 24, 25
8) 34, 8	16) 80, 35	24) 15, 60

Least Common Multiple

✎ Find the LCM for each number pair.

1) 2, 12	9) 11, 10	17) 12, 4, 24
2) 3, 18	10) 9, 36	18) 11, 7, 9
3) 16, 4	11) 19, 7	19) 5, 6, 30
4) 15, 20	12) 7, 9	20) 8, 32, 5
5) 6, 18	13) 30, 6	21) 4, 8, 6
6) 12, 6	14) 8, 2	22) 12, 8, 96
7) 25, 12	15) 20, 10, 15	23) 5, 15, 25
8) 8, 7	16) 12, 6, 18	24) 24, 2, 5

Answers of Worksheets – Chapter 3

Factoring Numbers

1) 1, 2, 7, 14

2) 1, 2, 3, 6, 9, 18

3) 1, 2, 4, 8, 16, 32

4) 1, 2, 3, 6, 7, 14, 21, 42

5) 1, 2, 3, 4, 6, 8, 12, 24

6) 1, 3, 5, 15, 25, 75

7) 1, 2, 3, 6, 11, 22, 33, 66

8) 1, 2, 3, 4, 5, 6, 10, 12, 15, 20, 30, 60

9) 1, 2, 19, 38

10) 1, 2, 4, 13, 26, 52

11) 1, 3, 13, 39

12) 1, 5, 7, 35

13) 1, 2, 3, 6, 9, 18, 27, 54

14) 1, 2, 11, 22

15) 1, 2, 3, 4, 6, 7, 12, 14, 21, 28, 42, 84

16) $2 \times 2 \times 3$

17) $2 \times 2 \times 3 \times 3$

18) 2×11

19) $3 \times 3 \times 5$

20) $2 \times 5 \times 5$

21) $2 \times 2 \times 2 \times 2 \times 2$

22) 7×7

23) 5×17

24) 2×47

Prime Factorization

1) 3. 5

2) 2. 11

3) 3. 3

4) 2. 2. 2. 3

5) 2. 2. 2. 2

6) 2. 17

7) 2. 2. 7

8) 2. 13

9) 2. 3. 11

10) 2. 2. 3. 3

11) 2. 7

12) 2. 2. 2. 7

13) 2. 2. 13

14) 2. 5. 7

15) 2. 2. 3. 7

16) 2. 11

17) 7. 13

18) 2. 3. 5

19) 2. 2. 2

20) 2. 2. 3

21) 3. 3. 7

22) 3. 11

23) 5. 7

24) 2. 3. 3. 3

Divisibility Rules

1) 10   <u>2</u> 3 4 <u>5</u> 6 7 8 9 <u>10</u>

2) 12   <u>2</u> <u>3</u> <u>4</u> 5 <u>6</u> 7 8 9 10

3) 24   <u>2</u> <u>3</u> <u>4</u> 5 <u>6</u> 7 <u>8</u> 9 10

4) 15   2 <u>3</u> 4 <u>5</u> 6 7 8 9 10

5) 30   <u>2</u> <u>3</u> 4 <u>5</u> <u>6</u> 7 8 9 <u>10</u>

6) 5   2 3 4 <u>5</u> 6 7 8 9 10

7) 32   <u>2</u> 3 <u>4</u> 5 6 7 <u>8</u> 9 10

8) 48   <u>2</u> <u>3</u> <u>4</u> 5 <u>6</u> 7 <u>8</u> 9 10

9) 16   <u>2</u> 3 <u>4</u> 5 6 7 <u>8</u> 9 10

10) 25   2 3 4 <u>5</u> 6 7 8 9 10

11) 35   2 3 4 <u>5</u> 6 <u>7</u> 8 9 10

12) 49   2 3 4 5 6 <u>7</u> 8 9 10

Greatest Common Factor

1) 10	7) 3	13) 4	19) 2
2) 2	8) 2	14) 10	20) 25
3) 5	9) 4	15) 2	21) 10
4) 12	10) 1	16) 5	22) 12
5) 1	11) 2	17) 1	23) 1
6) 3	12) 7	18) 5	24) 15

Least Common Multiple

1) 14	7) 300	13) 30	19) 30
2) 18	8) 56	14) 8	20) 160
3) 16	9) 110	15) 60	21) 24
4) 60	10) 36	16) 36	22) 96
5) 18	11) 133	17) 24	23) 75
6) 12	12) 63	18) 693	24) 120

Chapter 4: Fractions and Mixed Numbers

Topics that you'll learn in this chapter:

✓ Simplifying Fractions

✓ Add and Subtract Fractions with Like Denominators

✓ Compare Fractions with Like Denominators

✓ More than two Fractions with Like Denominators

✓ Add and Subtract Fractions with Unlike Denominators

✓ Ordering Fractions

✓ Add and Subtract Fractions with Denominators of 10, 100, and 1000

✓ Fractions to Mixed Numbers

✓ Mixed Numbers to Fractions

✓ Add and Subtract Mixed Numbers with Like Denominators

Simplifying Fractions

✍ Simplify the fractions.

1) $\frac{33}{63}$

2) $\frac{4}{10}$

3) $\frac{15}{20}$

4) $\frac{5}{30}$

5) $\frac{13}{26}$

6) $\frac{7}{49}$

7) $\frac{6}{21}$

8) $\frac{15}{45}$

9) $\frac{8}{10}$

10) $\frac{8}{56}$

11) $\frac{14}{42}$

12) $\frac{30}{20}$

13) $\frac{30}{42}$

14) $\frac{21}{28}$

15) $\frac{13}{65}$

16) $\frac{25}{40}$

17) $\frac{12}{32}$

18) $\frac{24}{64}$

19) $\frac{11}{99}$

20) $\frac{36}{48}$

21) $\frac{8}{72}$

22) $\frac{17}{34}$

Like Denominators

✎ Add fractions.

1) $\dfrac{2}{3} + \dfrac{1}{3}$

2) $\dfrac{2}{9} + \dfrac{7}{9}$

3) $\dfrac{5}{8} + \dfrac{6}{8}$

4) $\dfrac{1}{6} + \dfrac{3}{6}$

5) $\dfrac{4}{11} + \dfrac{3}{11}$

6) $\dfrac{3}{12} + \dfrac{2}{12}$

7) $\dfrac{1}{7} + \dfrac{3}{7}$

8) $\dfrac{5}{15} + \dfrac{7}{15}$

9) $\dfrac{5}{19} + \dfrac{10}{19}$

10) $\dfrac{4}{7} + \dfrac{4}{7}$

11) $\dfrac{3}{16} + \dfrac{7}{16}$

12) $\dfrac{8}{15} + \dfrac{10}{15}$

13) $\dfrac{11}{17} + \dfrac{6}{17}$

14) $\dfrac{7}{18} + \dfrac{5}{18}$

15) $\dfrac{7}{13} + \dfrac{1}{13}$

16) $\dfrac{10}{24} + \dfrac{11}{24}$

17) $\dfrac{12}{34} + \dfrac{11}{34}$

18) $\dfrac{4}{11} + \dfrac{5}{11}$

19) $\dfrac{12}{41} + \dfrac{11}{41}$

20) $\dfrac{8}{38} + \dfrac{15}{38}$

21) $\dfrac{17}{39} + \dfrac{2}{39}$

22) $\dfrac{7}{13} + \dfrac{6}{13}$

23) $\dfrac{4}{9} + \dfrac{2}{9}$

24) $\dfrac{5}{23} + \dfrac{2}{23}$

25) $\dfrac{8}{10} + \dfrac{1}{10}$

26) $\dfrac{7}{13} + \dfrac{1}{13}$

27) $\dfrac{4}{18} + \dfrac{3}{18}$

28) $\dfrac{9}{21} + \dfrac{12}{21}$

29) $\dfrac{4}{11} + \dfrac{4}{11}$

30) $\dfrac{12}{35} + \dfrac{5}{35}$

🖎 Subtract fractions.

1) $\dfrac{5}{7} - \dfrac{2}{7}$

2) $\dfrac{4}{5} - \dfrac{2}{5}$

3) $\dfrac{10}{13} - \dfrac{4}{13}$

4) $\dfrac{7}{9} - \dfrac{2}{9}$

5) $\dfrac{5}{10} - \dfrac{3}{10}$

6) $\dfrac{4}{7} - \dfrac{3}{7}$

7) $\dfrac{7}{17} - \dfrac{5}{17}$

8) $\dfrac{14}{15} - \dfrac{2}{15}$

9) $\dfrac{8}{21} - \dfrac{5}{21}$

10) $\dfrac{10}{12} - \dfrac{8}{12}$

11) $\dfrac{10}{14} - \dfrac{2}{14}$

12) $\dfrac{11}{21} - \dfrac{1}{21}$

13) $\dfrac{12}{29} - \dfrac{11}{29}$

14) $\dfrac{5}{36} - \dfrac{1}{36}$

15) $\dfrac{25}{27} - \dfrac{15}{27}$

16) $\dfrac{22}{45} - \dfrac{12}{45}$

17) $\dfrac{31}{39} - \dfrac{26}{39}$

18) $\dfrac{14}{26} - \dfrac{13}{26}$

19) $\dfrac{35}{47} - \dfrac{15}{47}$

20) $\dfrac{29}{34} - \dfrac{19}{34}$

21) $\dfrac{21}{38} - \dfrac{9}{38}$

22) $\dfrac{3}{9} - \dfrac{2}{9}$

23) $\dfrac{5}{6} - \dfrac{3}{6}$

24) $\dfrac{3}{5} - \dfrac{2}{5}$

25) $\dfrac{7}{14} - \dfrac{2}{14}$

26) $\dfrac{6}{42} - \dfrac{3}{42}$

27) $\dfrac{4}{23} - \dfrac{1}{23}$

28) $\dfrac{5}{16} - \dfrac{4}{16}$

29) $\dfrac{15}{55} - \dfrac{2}{55}$

30) $\dfrac{10}{27} - \dfrac{7}{27}$

Compare Fractions with Like Denominators

✐Evaluate and compare. Write < or > or =.

1) $\frac{1}{4} + \frac{2}{4}$ —— $\frac{1}{4}$

2) $\frac{4}{5} + \frac{1}{5}$ —— $\frac{3}{5}$

3) $\frac{5}{8} - \frac{3}{8}$ —— $\frac{6}{8}$

4) $\frac{8}{12} + \frac{7}{12}$ —— $\frac{4}{12}$

5) $\frac{4}{7} - \frac{3}{7}$ —— $\frac{4}{7}$

6) $\frac{9}{13} - \frac{4}{13}$ —— $\frac{3}{13}$

7) $\frac{3}{10} + \frac{1}{10}$ —— $\frac{1}{10}$

8) $\frac{12}{10} + \frac{2}{10}$ —— $\frac{7}{10}$

9) $\frac{15}{19} - \frac{3}{19}$ —— $\frac{15}{19}$

10) $\frac{18}{22} + \frac{4}{22}$ —— $\frac{17}{22}$

11) $\frac{10}{18} - \frac{4}{18}$ —— $\frac{15}{18}$

12) $\frac{27}{45} - \frac{11}{45}$ —— $\frac{20}{45}$

13) $\frac{25}{30} + \frac{5}{30}$ —— $\frac{18}{30}$

14) $\frac{20}{25} - \frac{3}{25}$ —— $\frac{9}{25}$

15) $\frac{45}{49} - \frac{25}{49}$ —— $\frac{37}{49}$

16) $\frac{32}{39} + \frac{12}{39}$ —— $\frac{18}{39}$

More Than Two Fractions with Like Denominators

✍ Add fractions.

1) $\dfrac{4}{8} + \dfrac{3}{8} + \dfrac{1}{8}$

2) $\dfrac{2}{5} + \dfrac{2}{5} + \dfrac{1}{5}$

3) $\dfrac{3}{10} + \dfrac{1}{10} + \dfrac{3}{10}$

4) $\dfrac{2}{7} + \dfrac{2}{7} + \dfrac{2}{7}$

5) $\dfrac{5}{14} + \dfrac{3}{14} + \dfrac{4}{14}$

6) $\dfrac{5}{21} + \dfrac{1}{21} + \dfrac{4}{21}$

7) $\dfrac{4}{11} + \dfrac{2}{11} + \dfrac{1}{11}$

8) $\dfrac{6}{19} + \dfrac{5}{19} + \dfrac{4}{19}$

9) $\dfrac{15}{31} + \dfrac{1}{31} + \dfrac{7}{31}$

10) $\dfrac{1}{14} + \dfrac{5}{14} + \dfrac{8}{14}$

11) $\dfrac{3}{25} + \dfrac{4}{25} + \dfrac{4}{25}$

12) $\dfrac{5}{20} + \dfrac{10}{20} + \dfrac{6}{20}$

13) $\dfrac{8}{39} + \dfrac{7}{39} + \dfrac{6}{39}$

14) $\dfrac{9}{29} + \dfrac{10}{29} + \dfrac{5}{29}$

15) $\dfrac{7}{24} + \dfrac{1}{24} + \dfrac{3}{24}$

16) $\dfrac{2}{13} + \dfrac{7}{13} + \dfrac{3}{13}$

Unlike Denominators

✍ Add fraction.

1) $\frac{1}{5} + \frac{1}{7}$

2) $\frac{3}{8} + \frac{1}{2}$

3) $\frac{3}{4} + \frac{1}{7}$

4) $\frac{1}{6} + \frac{2}{3}$

5) $\frac{2}{9} + \frac{1}{2}$

6) $\frac{3}{4} + \frac{2}{5}$

7) $\frac{16}{15} + \frac{3}{5}$

8) $\frac{3}{11} + \frac{1}{2}$

9) $\frac{3}{6} + \frac{2}{7}$

10) $\frac{1}{3} + \frac{1}{21}$

11) $\frac{2}{8} + \frac{1}{3}$

12) $\frac{5}{36} + \frac{2}{6}$

13) $\frac{3}{16} + \frac{1}{4}$

14) $\frac{5}{4} + \frac{1}{6}$

15) $\frac{1}{8} + \frac{2}{9}$

16) $\frac{2}{9} + \frac{1}{3}$

17) $\frac{3}{2} + \frac{2}{5}$

18) $\frac{2}{7} + \frac{1}{4}$

19) $\frac{1}{4} + \frac{1}{24}$

20) $\frac{13}{32} + \frac{3}{8}$

21) $\frac{3}{13} + \frac{1}{2}$

22) $\frac{2}{22} + \frac{1}{2}$

✎ Subtract fractions.

1) $\dfrac{3}{7} - \dfrac{1}{3}$

2) $\dfrac{3}{5} - \dfrac{1}{4}$

3) $\dfrac{1}{3} - \dfrac{1}{5}$

4) $\dfrac{6}{6} - \dfrac{3}{5}$

5) $\dfrac{3}{3} - \dfrac{3}{21}$

6) $\dfrac{15}{20} - \dfrac{1}{10}$

7) $\dfrac{3}{12} - \dfrac{1}{6}$

8) $\dfrac{8}{9} - \dfrac{2}{3}$

9) $\dfrac{13}{25} - \dfrac{1}{5}$

10) $\dfrac{1}{3} - \dfrac{1}{15}$

11) $\dfrac{4}{5} - \dfrac{2}{7}$

12) $\dfrac{1}{2} - \dfrac{2}{9}$

13) $\dfrac{3}{7} - \dfrac{1}{4}$

14) $\dfrac{5}{3} - \dfrac{1}{4}$

15) $\dfrac{1}{7} - \dfrac{2}{28}$

16) $\dfrac{1}{5} - \dfrac{6}{35}$

17) $\dfrac{29}{32} - \dfrac{3}{4}$

18) $\dfrac{4}{9} - \dfrac{1}{3}$

19) $\dfrac{13}{44} - \dfrac{2}{11}$

20) $\dfrac{1}{2} - \dfrac{4}{11}$

21) $\dfrac{3}{4} - \dfrac{2}{7}$

22) $\dfrac{4}{5} - \dfrac{1}{8}$

Ordering Fractions

✎ Order the fractions from least to greatest.

1) $\dfrac{1}{4}$, $\dfrac{1}{6}$, $\dfrac{1}{7}$, $\dfrac{1}{2}$ ____, ____, ____, ____

2) $\dfrac{1}{4}$, $\dfrac{1}{12}$, $\dfrac{3}{6}$, $\dfrac{1}{3}$ ____, ____, ____, ____

3) $\dfrac{5}{8}$, $\dfrac{2}{8}$, $\dfrac{12}{16}$, $\dfrac{5}{16}$ ____, ____, ____, ____

4) $\dfrac{2}{3}$, $\dfrac{5}{6}$, $\dfrac{3}{4}$, $\dfrac{7}{12}$ ____, ____, ____, ____

5) $\dfrac{1}{2}$, $\dfrac{3}{8}$, $\dfrac{5}{32}$, $\dfrac{1}{4}$ ____, ____, ____, ____

✎ Order the fractions from greatest to least.

6) $\dfrac{2}{5}$, $\dfrac{3}{8}$, $\dfrac{4}{12}$, $\dfrac{7}{11}$ ____, ____, ____, ____

7) $\dfrac{7}{10}$, $\dfrac{3}{5}$, $\dfrac{3}{4}$, $\dfrac{1}{2}$ ____, ____, ____, ____

8) $\dfrac{5}{7}$, $\dfrac{1}{5}$, $\dfrac{4}{12}$, $\dfrac{2}{3}$ ____, ____, ____, ____

9) $\dfrac{5}{6}$, $\dfrac{3}{8}$, $\dfrac{9}{16}$, $\dfrac{11}{12}$ ____, ____, ____, ____

10) $\dfrac{14}{30}$, $\dfrac{13}{14}$, $\dfrac{15}{28}$, $\dfrac{4}{15}$ ____, ____, ____, ____

Denominators of 10, 100, and 1000

✎ Add fractions.

1) $\dfrac{5}{10} + \dfrac{20}{100}$

2) $\dfrac{5}{10} + \dfrac{40}{100}$

3) $\dfrac{28}{100} + \dfrac{6}{10}$

4) $\dfrac{73}{100} + \dfrac{1}{10}$

5) $\dfrac{43}{100} + \dfrac{1}{10}$

6) $\dfrac{4}{10} + \dfrac{40}{100}$

7) $\dfrac{5}{100} + \dfrac{2}{10}$

8) $\dfrac{20}{100} + \dfrac{8}{10}$

9) $\dfrac{36}{100} + \dfrac{3}{10}$

10) $\dfrac{7}{10} + \dfrac{15}{100}$

11) $\dfrac{5}{10} + \dfrac{50}{100}$

12) $\dfrac{40}{100} + \dfrac{1}{10}$

13) $\dfrac{23}{100} + \dfrac{5}{10}$

14) $\dfrac{11}{100} + \dfrac{7}{10}$

15) $\dfrac{15}{100} + \dfrac{4}{10}$

16) $\dfrac{7}{10} + \dfrac{21}{100}$

17) $\dfrac{35}{100} + \dfrac{3}{10}$

18) $\dfrac{86}{100} + \dfrac{1}{10}$

✏ Subtract fractions.

1) $\dfrac{9}{10} - \dfrac{30}{100}$

2) $\dfrac{4}{10} - \dfrac{17}{100}$

3) $\dfrac{15}{100} - \dfrac{50}{1000}$

4) $\dfrac{85}{100} - \dfrac{150}{1000}$

5) $\dfrac{33}{100} - \dfrac{130}{1000}$

6) $\dfrac{40}{10} - \dfrac{380}{1000}$

7) $\dfrac{80}{100} - \dfrac{660}{1000}$

8) $\dfrac{80}{100} - \dfrac{5}{10}$

9) $\dfrac{460}{1000} - \dfrac{3}{10}$

10) $\dfrac{64}{100} - \dfrac{140}{1000}$

11) $\dfrac{8}{10} - \dfrac{25}{100}$

12) $\dfrac{45}{100} - \dfrac{3}{10}$

13) $\dfrac{40}{100} - \dfrac{2}{10}$

14) $\dfrac{600}{1000} - \dfrac{1}{100}$

15) $\dfrac{600}{1000} - \dfrac{50}{100}$

16) $\dfrac{670}{1000} - \dfrac{4}{10}$

17) $\dfrac{70}{100} - \dfrac{6}{10}$

18) $\dfrac{80}{100} - \dfrac{350}{1000}$

Fractions to Mixed Numbers

✍ Convert fractions to mixed numbers.

1) $\frac{7}{4}$

2) $\frac{44}{5}$

3) $\frac{27}{6}$

4) $\frac{22}{10}$

5) $\frac{9}{2}$

6) $\frac{46}{10}$

7) $\frac{28}{8}$

8) $\frac{13}{5}$

9) $\frac{22}{5}$

10) $\frac{16}{10}$

11) $\frac{14}{6}$

12) $\frac{30}{8}$

13) $\frac{11}{2}$

14) $\frac{33}{4}$

15) $\frac{52}{10}$

16) $\frac{14}{3}$

17) $\frac{51}{8}$

18) $\frac{29}{5}$

19) $\frac{19}{6}$

20) $\frac{13}{5}$

Mixed Numbers to Fractions

✍ Convert to fraction.

1) $2\frac{2}{7}$

2) $1\frac{3}{5}$

3) $7\frac{1}{4}$

4) $4\frac{4}{7}$

5) $4\frac{1}{4}$

6) $1\frac{3}{7}$

7) $4\frac{4}{9}$

8) $6\frac{9}{10}$

9) $7\frac{5}{6}$

10) $5\frac{10}{11}$

11) $2\frac{9}{20}$

12) $7\frac{2}{7}$

13) $4\frac{3}{5}$

14) $6\frac{1}{6}$

15) $9\frac{3}{4}$

16) $12\frac{2}{5}$

17) $11\frac{3}{7}$

18) $13\frac{6}{7}$

19) $4\frac{6}{7}$

20) $10\frac{2}{3}$

21) $11\frac{1}{5}$

22) $5\frac{2}{7}$

Add and Subtract Mixed Numbers

✐Add mixed numbers.

1) $2\frac{2}{3} + 7\frac{1}{2}$

10) $4\frac{2}{8} + 4\frac{1}{2}$

2) $5\frac{1}{2} + 5\frac{4}{5}$

11) $2\frac{5}{8} + 3\frac{1}{8}$

3) $7\frac{1}{5} + 3\frac{1}{2}$

12) $3\frac{2}{7} + 5\frac{1}{5}$

4) $5\frac{1}{2} + 4\frac{1}{3}$

13) $9\frac{1}{3} - 4\frac{2}{3}$

5) $5\frac{1}{3} - 2\frac{2}{3}$

14) $1\frac{2}{7} + 4\frac{1}{5}$

6) $8\frac{3}{15} - 3\frac{3}{5}$

15) $1\frac{1}{5} + 3\frac{1}{2}$

7) $8\frac{3}{7} - 4\frac{5}{7}$

16) $5\frac{1}{2} - 2\frac{2}{3}$

8) $4\frac{6}{5} - 1\frac{8}{15}$

17) $\frac{1}{2} + 4\frac{1}{4}$

9) $6\frac{21}{25} - 2\frac{12}{25}$

18) $4\frac{2}{3} + 3\frac{1}{6}$

Answers of Worksheets – Chapter 4

Simplifying Fractions

1) $\frac{11}{21}$

2) $\frac{2}{5}$

3) $\frac{3}{4}$

4) $\frac{1}{6}$

5) $\frac{1}{2}$

6) $\frac{1}{7}$

7) $\frac{2}{7}$

8) $\frac{1}{3}$

9) $\frac{4}{5}$

10) $\frac{1}{7}$

11) $\frac{1}{3}$

12) $\frac{3}{2}$

13) $\frac{5}{7}$

14) $\frac{3}{4}$

15) $\frac{1}{5}$

16) $\frac{5}{8}$

17) $\frac{3}{8}$

18) $\frac{3}{8}$

19) $\frac{1}{9}$

20) $\frac{3}{4}$

21) $\frac{1}{9}$

22) $\frac{1}{2}$

Add Fractions with Like Denominators

1) 1

2) 1

3) $\frac{11}{8}$

4) $\frac{4}{6}$

5) $\frac{7}{11}$

6) $\frac{5}{12}$

7) $\frac{4}{7}$

8) $\frac{12}{15}$

9) $\frac{15}{19}$

10) $\frac{8}{7}$

11) $\frac{10}{16}$

12) $\frac{18}{15}$

13) 1

14) $\frac{12}{18}$

15) $\frac{8}{13}$

16) $\frac{21}{24}$

17) $\frac{23}{34}$

18) $\frac{9}{11}$

19) $\frac{23}{41}$

20) $\frac{23}{38}$

21) $\frac{19}{39}$

22) 1

23) $\frac{6}{9}$

24) $\frac{7}{23}$

25) $\frac{9}{10}$

26) $\frac{8}{13}$

27) $\frac{7}{18}$

28) 1

29) $\frac{8}{11}$

30) $\frac{17}{35}$

Subtract Fractions with Like Denominators

1) $\frac{3}{7}$

2) $\frac{2}{5}$

3) $\frac{6}{13}$

4) $\frac{5}{9}$

5) $\frac{7}{10}$

6) $\frac{1}{7}$

7) $\frac{2}{17}$

8) $\frac{12}{15}$

9) $\frac{3}{21}$

10) $\frac{2}{12}$

11) $\frac{8}{14}$

12) $\frac{9}{21}$

13) $\frac{1}{29}$

14) $\frac{4}{36}$

15) $\frac{10}{27}$

16) $\frac{10}{45}$ 21) $\frac{12}{38}$ 26) $\frac{3}{42}$

17) $\frac{5}{39}$ 22) $\frac{1}{9}$ 27) $\frac{3}{23}$

18) $\frac{1}{26}$ 23) $\frac{2}{6}$ 28) $\frac{1}{16}$

19) $\frac{20}{47}$ 24) $\frac{1}{5}$ 29) $\frac{13}{55}$

20) $\frac{10}{34}$ 25) $\frac{5}{14}$ 30) $\frac{3}{27}$

Compare Fractions with Like Denominators

1) $\frac{3}{4} > \frac{1}{4}$ 7) $\frac{4}{10} > \frac{1}{10}$ 13) $1 > \frac{18}{30}$

2) $1 > \frac{3}{5}$ 8) $\frac{14}{10} > \frac{7}{10}$ 14) $\frac{17}{25} > \frac{9}{25}$

3) $\frac{2}{8} < \frac{6}{8}$ 9) $\frac{12}{19} < \frac{15}{19}$ 15) $\frac{20}{49} < \frac{37}{49}$

4) $\frac{15}{12} > \frac{4}{12}$ 10) $1 > \frac{17}{22}$ 16) $\frac{44}{39} > \frac{18}{39}$

5) $\frac{1}{7} < \frac{4}{7}$ 11) $\frac{6}{18} < \frac{15}{18}$

6) $\frac{5}{13} > \frac{3}{13}$ 12) $\frac{16}{45} < \frac{20}{45}$

More Than Two Fractions with Like Denominators

1) 1 5) $\frac{12}{14}$ 9) $\frac{23}{31}$ 13) $\frac{21}{39}$

2) 1 6) $\frac{10}{21}$ 10) 1 14) $\frac{24}{29}$

3) $\frac{7}{8}$ 7) $\frac{7}{11}$ 11) $\frac{11}{25}$ 15) $\frac{11}{24}$

4) $\frac{6}{7}$ 8) $\frac{16}{19}$ 12) $\frac{21}{20}$ 16) $\frac{12}{13}$

Add fractions with unlike denominators

1) $\frac{12}{35}$ 6) $\frac{23}{20}$ 11) $\frac{7}{12}$ 16) $\frac{5}{9}$

2) $\frac{7}{8}$ 7) $\frac{25}{15}$ 12) $\frac{17}{36}$ 17) $\frac{19}{10}$

3) $\frac{25}{28}$ 8) $\frac{17}{22}$ 13) $\frac{7}{16}$ 18) $\frac{15}{28}$

4) $\frac{5}{6}$ 9) $\frac{11}{14}$ 14) $\frac{17}{12}$ 19) $\frac{7}{24}$

5) $\frac{13}{18}$ 10) $\frac{8}{21}$ 15) $\frac{25}{72}$ 20) $\frac{25}{32}$

21) $\frac{19}{26}$ 22) $\frac{13}{22}$

Subtract fractions with unlike denominators

1) $\frac{2}{21}$ 7) $\frac{1}{12}$ 13) $\frac{5}{28}$ 19) $\frac{5}{44}$

2) $\frac{7}{20}$ 8) $\frac{2}{9}$ 14) $\frac{17}{12}$ 20) $\frac{3}{22}$

3) $\frac{2}{15}$ 9) $\frac{8}{25}$ 15) $\frac{1}{14}$ 21) $\frac{13}{28}$

4) $\frac{2}{5}$ 10) $\frac{4}{15}$ 16) $\frac{1}{35}$ 22) $\frac{27}{40}$

5) $\frac{6}{7}$ 11) $\frac{18}{35}$ 17) $\frac{5}{32}$

6) $\frac{13}{20}$ 12) $\frac{5}{18}$ 18) $\frac{1}{9}$

Ordering Fractions

1) $\frac{1}{7}, \frac{1}{6}, \frac{1}{4}, \frac{1}{2}$ 5) $\frac{5}{32}, \frac{1}{4}, \frac{3}{8}, \frac{1}{2}$ 9) $\frac{11}{12}, \frac{5}{6}, \frac{9}{16}, \frac{3}{8}$

2) $\frac{1}{12}, \frac{1}{4}, \frac{1}{3}, \frac{3}{6},$ 6) $\frac{7}{11}, \frac{2}{5}, \frac{3}{8}, \frac{4}{12}$ 10) $\frac{13}{14}, \frac{15}{28}, \frac{14}{30}, \frac{4}{15}$

3) $\frac{2}{8}, \frac{5}{16}, \frac{5}{8}, \frac{12}{16}$ 7) $\frac{3}{4}, \frac{7}{10}, \frac{3}{5}, \frac{1}{2}$

4) $\frac{7}{12}, \frac{2}{3}, \frac{3}{4}, \frac{5}{6}$ 8) $\frac{5}{7}, \frac{2}{3}, \frac{4}{12}, \frac{1}{5}$

Add fractions with denominators of 10, 100, and 1000

1) $\frac{7}{10}$ 6) $\frac{4}{5}$ 11) 1 16) $\frac{91}{100}$

2) $\frac{9}{10}$ 7) $\frac{1}{4}$ 12) $\frac{1}{2}$ 17) $\frac{13}{20}$

3) $\frac{22}{25}$ 8) 1 13) $\frac{73}{100}$ 18) $\frac{24}{25}$

4) $\frac{83}{100}$ 9) $\frac{33}{50}$ 14) $\frac{81}{100}$

5) $\frac{53}{100}$ 10) $\frac{17}{20}$ 15) $\frac{11}{20}$

Subtract fractions with denominators of 10, 100, and 1000

1) $\frac{3}{5}$ 4) $\frac{7}{10}$ 7) $\frac{7}{50}$ 10) $\frac{1}{2}$

2) $\frac{23}{100}$ 5) $\frac{1}{5}$ 8) $\frac{3}{10}$ 11) $\frac{11}{20}$

3) $\frac{1}{10}$ 6) $\frac{181}{50}$ 9) $\frac{4}{25}$ 12) $\frac{3}{20}$

13) $\frac{1}{5}$ 15) $\frac{1}{10}$ 17) $\frac{1}{10}$

14) $\frac{59}{100}$ 16) $\frac{27}{100}$ 18) $\frac{9}{20}$

Fractions to Mixed Numbers

1) $1\frac{3}{4}$ 6) $4\frac{3}{5}$ 11) $2\frac{1}{3}$ 16) $4\frac{2}{3}$

2) $8\frac{4}{5}$ 7) $3\frac{1}{2}$ 12) $3\frac{3}{4}$ 17) $6\frac{3}{8}$

3) $4\frac{1}{2}$ 8) $2\frac{3}{5}$ 13) $5\frac{1}{2}$ 18) $5\frac{4}{5}$

4) $2\frac{1}{5}$ 9) $4\frac{2}{5}$ 14) $8\frac{1}{4}$ 19) $3\frac{1}{6}$

5) $4\frac{1}{2}$ 10) $1\frac{3}{5}$ 15) $5\frac{1}{5}$ 20) $2\frac{3}{5}$

Mixed Numbers to Fractions

1) $\frac{16}{7}$ 7) $\frac{40}{9}$ 13) $\frac{23}{5}$ 19) $\frac{34}{7}$

2) $\frac{8}{5}$ 8) $\frac{69}{10}$ 14) $\frac{37}{6}$ 20) $\frac{32}{3}$

3) $\frac{29}{4}$ 9) $\frac{47}{6}$ 15) $\frac{39}{4}$ 21) $\frac{56}{5}$

4) $\frac{32}{7}$ 10) $\frac{65}{11}$ 16) $\frac{62}{5}$ 22) $\frac{37}{7}$

5) $\frac{17}{4}$ 11) $\frac{49}{20}$ 17) $\frac{80}{7}$

6) $\frac{10}{7}$ 12) $\frac{51}{7}$ 18) $\frac{97}{7}$

Add and Subtract Mixed Numbers with Like Denominators

1) $10\frac{1}{6}$ 6) $4\frac{3}{5}$ 11) $5\frac{3}{4}$ 16) $2\frac{5}{6}$

2) $11\frac{3}{10}$ 7) $3\frac{5}{7}$ 12) $8\frac{17}{35}$ 17) $4\frac{3}{4}$

3) $10\frac{7}{10}$ 8) $3\frac{2}{3}$ 13) $4\frac{2}{3}$ 18) $7\frac{5}{6}$

4) $9\frac{5}{6}$ 9) $4\frac{9}{25}$ 14) $5\frac{17}{35}$

5) $2\frac{2}{3}$ 10) $8\frac{3}{4}$ 15) $4\frac{7}{10}$

Chapter 5: Decimals

Topics that you'll learn in this chapter:

✓ Adding and Subtracting Decimals

✓ Multiplying and Dividing Decimals

✓ Order and Comparing Decimals

✓ Round decimals

✓ Comparing Decimals

Adding and Subtracting Decimals

✎ Add and subtract decimals.

1) $\begin{array}{r} 18.14 \\ -\ 11.18 \\ \hline \end{array}$

4) $\begin{array}{r} 46.18 \\ -\ 23.45 \\ \hline \end{array}$

2) $\begin{array}{r} 39.72 \\ +\ 23.67 \\ \hline \end{array}$

5) $\begin{array}{r} 80.30 \\ +\ 27.97 \\ \hline \end{array}$

3) $\begin{array}{r} 83.36 \\ +\ 12.18 \\ \hline \end{array}$

6) $\begin{array}{r} 66.68 \\ -\ 21.39 \\ \hline \end{array}$

✎ Solve.

7) ____ $+ 1.3 = 6.7$

10) $3.7 +$ ____ $= 14.4$

8) $4.2 +$ ____ $= 10.6$

11) ____ $+ 5.1 = 10.7$

9) $8.9 +$ ____ $= 18$

12) ____ $+ 9.9 = 15.2$

✎ Order each set of numbers from least to greatest.

1) $0.3, 0.63, 0.33, 0.88, 0.46$ ___, ___, ___, ___, ___, ___

2) $4.2, 5.4, 4.35, 6.86, 4.80$ ___, ___, ___, ___, ___, ___

3) $1.2, 1.1, 0.8, 0.56, 0.23$ ___, ___, ___, ___, ___, ___

4) $1.6, 4.4, 1.2, 4.2, 1.74, 3.45$ ___, ___, ___, ___, ___, ___

5) $4.6, 7.2, 4.5, 6.7, 3.3, 3.43$ ___, ___, ___, ___, ___, ___

6) $0.78, 0.98, 0.23, 1.06, 2.2$ ___, ___, ___, ___, ___, ___

Multiplying and Dividing Decimals

✍ Find each product.

1) $\begin{array}{r} 2.4 \\ \times\ 1.3 \\ \hline \end{array}$

4) $\begin{array}{r} 3.9 \\ \times\ 5.7 \\ \hline \end{array}$

7) $\begin{array}{r} 3.7 \\ \times\ 7.3 \\ \hline \end{array}$

2) $\begin{array}{r} 6.7 \\ \times\ 4.8 \\ \hline \end{array}$

5) $\begin{array}{r} 11.1 \\ \times\ 9.6 \\ \hline \end{array}$

8) $\begin{array}{r} 98.20 \\ \times\ 100 \\ \hline \end{array}$

3) $\begin{array}{r} 1.5 \\ \times\ 1.3 \\ \hline \end{array}$

6) $\begin{array}{r} 2.5 \\ \times\ 5.3 \\ \hline \end{array}$

9) $\begin{array}{r} 10.12 \\ \times\ 5.9 \\ \hline \end{array}$

✍ Find each quotient.

10) $2.5 \div 0.98$

15) $9.2 \div 100$

11) $18.4 \div 2.8$

16) $6.24 \div 10$

12) $27.82 \div 6.7$

17) $8.5 \div 100$

13) $8.5 \div 5.2$

18) $7.14 \div 1.34$

14) $1.9 \div 10$

19) $16.24 \div 100$

Rounding Decimals

✐ Round each decimal number to the nearest place indicated.

1) 0.2<u>4</u>

2) 4.<u>0</u>3

3) 6.<u>6</u>12

4) 0.<u>2</u>89

5) <u>6</u>.34

6) 0.2<u>9</u>

7) 9.<u>2</u>1

8) <u>7</u>.1260

9) 4.4<u>2</u>9

10) 6.<u>3</u>912

11) <u>3</u>.8

12) <u>3</u>.3529

13) 7.<u>8</u>87

14) 2.<u>5</u>3

15) 5<u>0</u>.96

16) 6<u>5</u>.84

17) 35.<u>7</u>9

18) 83<u>5</u>.885

19) 4<u>6</u>.3

20) 3<u>5</u>.81

21) <u>7</u>.308

22) 9<u>6</u>.2

23) 216.<u>5</u>32

24) 6.<u>0</u>9

Simplifying Ratios

✍ Reduce each ratio.

1) 16: 64

2) 10: 30

3) 7: 14

4) 21: 18

5) 30: 35

6) 18: 14

7) 400: 20

8) 9: 6

9) 20: 16

10) 9: 18

11) 40: 56

12) 4: 36

13) 10: 15

14) 12: 30

15) 48: 8

16) 20: 40

17) 4: 44

18) 5: 20

19) 2: 50

20) 3: 30

21) 9: 27

22) 16: 72

23) 51: 60

24) 10: 100

Writing Ratios

✍ Express each ratio as a rate and unite rate.

1) 150 miles on 5 gallons of gas.

2) 81 dollars for 9 books.

3) 300 miles on 30 gallons of gas

4) 45 inches of snow in 9 hours

✍ Express each ratio as a fraction in the simplest form.

5) 5 feet out of 50 feet

6) 10 cakes out of 35 cakes

7) 24 dimes t0 45 dimes

8) 16 dimes out of 56 coins

9) 11 cups to 77 cups

10) 24 gallons to 36 gallons

11) 21 miles out of 72 miles

12) 8 blue cars out of 20 cars

13) 10 pennies to 100 pennies

14) 12 beetles out of 60 insects

15) 13 dimes to 39 dimes

16) 25 red cars out of 100 cars

Comparing Decimals

✍ Write the correct comparison symbol (>, < or =).

1) 0.26 ___ 2.4

2) 1.5 ___ 1.25

3) 7.1 ___ 7.1

4) 3.43 ___ 34.3

5) 4.65 ___ 0.465

6) 8.2 ___ 8

7) 8.1 ___ 0.81

8) 7.23 ___ 0.723

9) 6 ___ 0.6

10) 5.35 ___ 0.535

11) 13.3 ___ 13.5

12) 3.66 ___ 3.67

13) 6.08 ___ 6.22

14) 6.11 ___ 0.611

15) 7.89 ___ 7.86

16) 1.52 ___ 1.57

17) 3.52 ___ 0.352

18) 0.54 ___ 0.054

19) 19.4 ___ 19.4

20) 0.05 ___ 0.50

21) 0.69 ___ 0.7

22) 0.4 ___ 0.04

23) 0.30 ___ 0.3

24) 1.29 ___ 12.9

Answers of Worksheets – Chapter 5

Adding and Subtracting Decimals

1) 6.96	4) 22.73	7) 5.4	10) 10.7
2) 63.39	5) 108.27	8) 6.4	11) 5.6
3) 95.54	6) 45.29	9) 9.1	12) 5.3

Order and Comparing Decimals

1) 0.3, 0.33, 0.46, 0.63, 0.88	4) 1.2, 1.4, 1.6, 1.74, 4.2, 3.45
2) 4.2, 4.35, 4.80, 5.4, 6.86	5) 3.3, 3.43, 4.5, 4.6, 6.7, 7.2
3) 0.23, 0.56, 0.8, 1.1, 1.2	6) 0.23, 0.78, 0.98, 1.06, 2.2

Multiplying and Dividing Decimals

1) 3.12	6) 13.25	11) 6.571…	16) 0.624
2) 32.16	7) 27.01	12) 4.152…	17) 0.085
3) 1.95	8) 9,820	13) 1.634…	18) 5.328
4) 22.23	9) 59.708	14) 0.19	19) 0.1624
5) 106.56	10) 2.551…	15) 0.092	

Rounding Decimals

1) 0.2	7) 9.2	13) 7.9	19) 46
2) 4.0	8) 7	14) 2.5	20) 36
3) 6.6	9) 4.43	15) 51	21) 7
4) 0.3	10) 6.4	16) 66	22) 96
5) 6	11) 4	17) 35.8	23) 216.5
6) 0.3	12) 3	18) 836	24) 6.1

Comparing Decimals

1) 0.26 < 2.4	9) 6 > 0.6	17) 3.52 > 0.352
2) 1.5 > 1.25	10) 5.35 > 0.535	18) 0.54 > 0.054
3) 7.1 = 7.1	11) 13.3 < 13.5	19) 19.4 = 19.4
4) 3.43 < 34.3	12) 3.66 < 3.67	20) 0.05 < 0.50
5) 4.65 > 0.465	13) 6.08 < 6.22	21) 0.69 < 0.7
6) 8.2 > 8	14) 6.11 > 0.611	22) 0.4 > 0.04
7) 8.1 > 0.81	15) 7.89 > 7.86	23) 0.30 = 0.3
8) 7.23 > 0.73	16) 1.52 < 1.57	24) 1.29 < 12.9

Chapter 6: Ratios and rates

Topics that you'll learn in this chapter:

✓ Simplifying Ratios

✓ Writing Ratios

✓ Create a Proportion

✓ Proportional Ratios

✓ Ratio and Rates Word Problems

✓ Similar Figures

✓ Similar Figure Word Problems (Scale drawings: word problems)

Create a Proportion

✍ Create proportion from the given set of numbers.

1) 1, 12, 3, 4

2) 10, 110, 1, 11

3) 3, 9, 7, 21

4) 2, 5, 8, 20

5) 7, 2, 28, 8

6) 2, 3, 1, 6

7) 15, 5, 12, 4

8) 7, 2, 35, 10

9) 3, 24, 16, 2

10) 9, 27, 1, 3

11) 4, 1, 5, 20

12) 9, 16, 27, 48

Proportional Ratios

✍ Solve each proportion.

1) $\frac{3}{6} = \frac{2}{d}$

2) $\frac{k}{5} = \frac{4}{10}$

3) $\frac{20}{5} = \frac{6}{x}$

4) $\frac{x}{3} = \frac{1}{6}$

5) $\frac{d}{3} = \frac{3}{9}$

6) $\frac{15}{7} = \frac{30}{x}$

7) $\frac{8}{10} = \frac{k}{30}$

8) $\frac{100}{25} = \frac{10}{d}$

9) $\frac{x}{14} = \frac{6}{21}$

10) $\frac{15}{3} = \frac{x}{2}$

11) $\frac{12}{x} = \frac{12}{4}$

12) $\frac{x}{4} = \frac{36}{18}$

13) $\frac{40}{10} = \frac{k}{20}$

14) $\frac{36}{6} = \frac{18}{d}$

15) $\frac{x}{8} = \frac{20}{10}$

16) $\frac{9}{7} = \frac{k}{7}$

17) $\frac{20}{15} = \frac{15}{d}$

18) $\frac{40}{x} = \frac{20}{3}$

19) $\frac{d}{6} = \frac{18}{12}$

20) $\frac{k}{8} = \frac{8}{4}$

21) $\frac{12}{6} = \frac{x}{7}$

22) $\frac{30}{10} = \frac{k}{20}$

23) $\frac{13}{26} = \frac{x}{4}$

24) $\frac{8}{22} = \frac{x}{11}$

Similar Figures

Each pair of figures is similar. Find the missing side.

1)

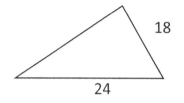 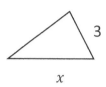

2)

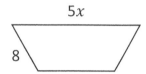 

3)

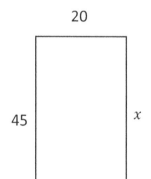 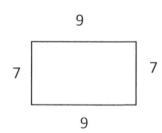

Word Problems

✎Solve.

1) In a party, 10 soft drinks are required for every 24 guests. If there are 480 guests, how many soft drinks is required?

2) In Jack's class, 24 of the students are tall and 15 are short. In Michael's class 56 students are tall and 35 students are short. Which class has a higher ratio of tall to short students?

3) Are these ratios equivalent?

10 cards to 70 animals 13 marbles to 91 marbles

4) The price of 5 apples at the Quick Market is $2.45. The price of 8 of the same apples at Walmart is $4.16. Which place is the better buy?

5) The bakers at a Bakery can make 200 bagels in 5 hours. How many bagels can they bake in 12 hours? What is that rate per hour?

✎Answer each question and round your answer to the nearest whole number.

6) If a 48.9 ft tall flagpole casts a 280.98 ft long shadow, then how long is the shadow that a 6.3 ft tall woman casts?

7) A model igloo has a scale of 1 in: 4 ft. If the real igloo is 24 ft wide, then how wide is the model igloo?

8) If a 45 ft tall tree casts a 9 ft long shadow, then how tall is an adult giraffe that casts a 6 ft shadow?

9) Find the distance between San Joe and Mount Pleasant if they are 3 cm apart on a map with a scale of 1 cm: 4 km.

10) A telephone booth that is 14 ft tall casts a shadow that is 7 ft long. Find the height of a lawn ornament that casts a 3 ft shadow.

Answers of Worksheets – Chapter 6

Simplifying Ratios

1) 2: 8
2) 1: 3
3) 1: 7
4) 7: 6
5) 6: 7
6) 9: 7

7) 20: 1
8) 3: 2
9) 5: 4
10) 1: 2
11) 5: 7
12) 1: 9

13) 2: 3
14) 2: 5
15) 6: 1
16) 1: 2
17) 1: 11
18) 1: 4

19) 1: 25
20) 1: 10
21) 1: 3
22) 2: 9
23) 17: 20
24) 1: 10

Writing Ratios

1) $\frac{150 \text{ miles}}{5 \text{ gallons}}$, 30 miles per gallon

2) $\frac{81 \text{ dollars}}{9 \text{ books}}$, 9.00 dollars per book

3) $\frac{300 \text{ miles}}{30 \text{ gallons}}$, 10 miles per gallon

4) $\frac{45" \text{ of snow}}{9 \text{ hours}}$, 5 inches of snow per hour

5) $\frac{1}{10}$
6) $\frac{2}{7}$
7) $\frac{8}{15}$

8) $\frac{2}{7}$
9) $\frac{1}{7}$
10) $\frac{2}{3}$

11) $\frac{7}{24}$
12) $\frac{2}{5}$
13) $\frac{1}{10}$

14) $\frac{1}{5}$
15) $\frac{1}{3}$
16) $\frac{1}{4}$

Create Proportion

1) 1: 4 = 3: 12
2) 10: 110 = 1: 11
3) 7: 3 = 21: 9
4) 5: 2 = 15: 6

5) 7: 2 =28: 8
6) 6: 3 = 2: 1
7) 12: 15 = 4: 5
8) 7: 2 = 35: 10

9) 2: 3 = 16: 24
10) 27: 9 = 3: 1
11) 4: 1 = 20: 5
12) 27: 9 = 48: 16

Proportional Ratios

1) 4
2) 2
3) 1.5
4) 0.5
5) 1
6) 14

7) 24
8) 2.5
9) 4
10) 10
11) 4
12) 8

13) 80
14) 3
15) 16
16) 9
17) 11.25
18) 6

19) 9
20) 16
21) 14
22) 60
23) 2
24) 4

Similar Figures

1) 4
2) 2
3) 45

Word Problems

1) 200

2) The ratio for both classes is equal to 8 to 5.

3) Yes! Both ratios are 1 to 7

4) The price at the Quick Market is a better buy.

5) 480, the rate is 40 per hour.

6) 36.2 ft

7) 6 in

8) 30 ft

9) 12 km

10) 6 ft

Chapter 7: Algebra

Topics that you'll learn in this chapter:

- ✓ Find a Rule between input and output

- ✓ Variables and Expressions

- ✓ Evaluating Variable

- ✓ Evaluating Two Variables

- ✓ Solve Equations

Find a Rule

✎ Complete the output.

1- **Rule:** the output is $x - 15$

Input	x	19	28	42	45	56
Output	y					

2- **Rule:** the output is $x \times 28$

Input	x	2	4	6	8	30
Output	y					

3- **Rule:** the output is $x \div 7$

Input	x	469	245	280	196	147
Output	y					

✎ Find a rule to write an expression.

4- **Rule:** _____

Input	x	8	16	20	28
Output	y	24	48	60	84

5- **Rule:** _____

Input	x	8	21	35	49
Output	y	16	29	43	57

6- **Rule:** _____

Input	x	99	162	261	288
Output	y	11	18	29	32

Variables and Expressions

✎ Write a verbal expression for each algebraic expression.

1) $2a - 4b$

2) $6c^2 + 2d$

3) $x - 17$

4) $\frac{80}{5}$

5) $a^2 + b^3$

6) $2x + 4$

7) $x^2 - 10y + 18$

8) $x^3 + 9y^2 - 4$

9) $\frac{1}{3} x + \frac{3}{4} y - 6$

10) $\frac{1}{5} (x + 8) - 10y$

✎ Write an algebraic expression for each verbal expression.

11) 9 less than h

12) The product of 10 and b

13) The 20 divided by K

14) The product of 5 and the third power of x

15) 10 more than h to the fifth power

16) 20 more than twice d

17) One fourth the square of b

18) The difference of 23 and 4 times a number

19) 60 more than the cube of a number

20) Three-quarters the cube of a number

Evaluating Variable

✎Simplify each algebraic expression.

1) $12 - x$, $x = 4$

2) $x + 10$, $x = 1$

3) $5x + 7$, $x = -2$

4) $2x + (-7)$, $x = -3$

5) $3x - 16$, $x = 2$

6) $5x + 6$, $x = -2$

7) $10 + 9x - 16$, $x = 2$

8) $11 - 2x$, $x = 7$

9) $\frac{40}{x} - 3$, $x = 5$

10) $(-13) + \frac{x}{2} + 2x$, $x = 8$

11) $(-8) + \frac{x}{6}$, $x = 42$

12) $\left(-\frac{20}{x}\right) - 8 + 9x$, $x = 2$

13) $\left(-\frac{27}{x}\right) - 9 + 5x$, $x = 3$

14) $(-4) + \frac{x}{5}$, $x = 25$

15) $5(15x + 10)$, $x = -1$

16) $12x + 14x - 20 + 2$,

$x = 1$

17) $\left(-\frac{12}{x}\right) + 12 + 3x$,

$x = 3$

18) $4(-3a + 6a)$,

$a = 4$

19) $15 - 6x + 17 - 2x$,

$x = 5$

20) $19x - 16 - 4x$,

$x = 3$

21) $20 - 3(3x + x)$, $x = 1$

Solve Equations

✎ Solve each equation.

1) $2x + 5 = 15$

2) $25 = (-5) + 2x$

3) $6x = 66$

4) $64 = 4x$

5) $(-6) = 16 + 2x$

6) $7 + 2x = (-3)$

7) $20x = 140$

8) $20 = 2x + 4$

9) $(-36) + x = (-20)$

10) $9x = 63$

11) $2x - 12 = (-46)$

12) $x - 13 = (-25)$

13) $(-60) = x - 45$

14) $24 = 3x$

15) $2x = 34$

16) $99 = 9x$

17) $x - 140 = 20$

18) $9x = 81$

19) $32 = 8x$

20) $2x = 72$

21) $2x + 28 = 40$

22) $2x - 15 = 31$

23) $45 + 2x - 21 = 0$

24) $90x = 900$

Answers of Worksheets – Chapter 7

Find a Rule

1)

Input	x	19	28	42	45	56
Output	y	4	13	27	30	41

2)

Input	x	2	4	6	8	30
Output	y	56	112	168	224	840

3)

Input	x	469	245	280	196	147
Output	y	67	35	40	28	21

4) $y = 3x$ 5) $y = x + 8$ 6) $y = x \div 9$

Variables and Expressions

1) 2 times a minus 4 times b

2) 6 times c squared plus 2 times d

3) a number minus 17

4) the quotient of 80 and 5

5) a squared plus b cubed

6) the product of 2 and x plus 4

7) x squared plus the product of 10 and y plus 18

8) x cubed plus the product of 9 and y squared minus the product of 4 and y

9) the sum of one–thirds of x and three–quarters of y, minus 6

10) one–sixth of the sum of x and 8 minus the product of 10 and y

11) $9 < h$

12) $10b$

13) $\frac{20}{K}$

14) $5x^3$

15) $10 > h^5$

16) $2d < 20$

17) $\frac{1}{4}b^2$

18) $23 - 4a$

19) $60 > a^3$

20) $\frac{3}{4}x^3$

Evaluating Variable

1) 8

2) 11

3) −3

4) −13

5) −10

6) −4

7) 12

8) −3

9) 5

10) 7

11) −1

12) 0

13) −3

14) 1

15) −25

16) 8

17) 17

18) 48

19) −8

20) 29

21) 8

Solve Equations

1) 5

2) 15

3) 11

4) 16

5) − 11

6) − 5

7) 7

8) 8

9) 16

10) 7

11) − 17

12) − 12

13) − 15

14) 8

15) 17

16) 11

17) 160

18) 9

19) 4

20) 36

21) 6

22) 23

23) −12

24) 10

Chapter 8: Measurement

Topics that you'll learn in this chapter:

- ✓ Reference Measurement

- ✓ Metric Length

- ✓ Customary Length

- ✓ Metric Capacity

- ✓ Customary Capacity

- ✓ Metric Weight and Mass

- ✓ Customary Weight and Mass

- ✓ Time

- ✓ Add Money Amounts

- ✓ Subtract Money Amounts

- ✓ Money: Word Problems

Reference Measurement

LENGTH

Customary	Metric
1 mile (mi) = 1,760 yards (yd)	1 kilometer (km) = 1,000 meters (m)
1 yard (yd) = 3 feet (ft)	1 meter (m) = 100 centimeters (cm)
1 foot (ft) = 12 inches (in.)	1 centimeter(cm)= 10 millimeters(mm)

VOLUME AND CAPACITY

Customary	Metric
1 gallon (gal) = 4 quarts (qt)	1 liter (L) = 1,000 milliliters (mL)
1 quart (qt) = 2 pints (pt.)	
1 pint (pt.) = 2 cups (c)	
1 cup (c) = 8 fluid ounces (Fl oz)	

WEIGHT AND MASS

Customary	Metric
1 ton (T) = 2,000 pounds (lb.)	1 kilogram (kg) = 1,000 grams (g)
1 pound (lb.) = 16 ounces (oz)	1 gram (g) = 1,000 milligrams (mg)

Time

1 year = 12 months

1 year = 52 weeks

1 week = 7 days

1 day = 24 hours

1 hour = 60 minutes

1 minute = 60 seconds

Metric Length Measurement

✍ Convert to the units.

1) 200 mm = _____ cm

2) 4 m = _____ mm

3) 5 m = _____ cm

4) 6 km = _____ m

5) 8,000mm = _____ m

6) 900 cm = _____ m

7) 11 m = _____ cm

8) 2,000 mm = _____ cm

9) 4,000 mm = _____ m

10) 6 km = _____ mm

11) 12 km = _____ m

12) 40 m = _____ cm

13) 8,000 m = _____ km

14) 9,000 m = _____ km

Customary Length Measurement

✍ Convert to the units.

1) 6 ft = _____ in

2) 3 ft = _____ in

3) 3 yd = _____ ft

4) 5 yd = _____ ft

5) 3 yd = _____ in

6) 36 in = _____ ft

7) 252 in = ____ yd

8) 180in = _____ yd

9) 20yd = _____ in

10) 58yd = _____ in

11) 81ft = _____ yd

12) 150ft = _____ yd

13) 96in = _____ ft

14) 60 yd = _____ feet

Metric Capacity Measurement

✎ Convert the following measurements.

1) 40 l = _____ ml

2) 6 l = _____ ml

3) 40 l = _____ ml

4) 32 l = _____ ml

5) 27 l = _____ ml

6) 13 l = _____ ml

7) 80,000 l = _____ l

8) 56,000mml = _____ l

9) 95,000ml = _____ l

10) 4,000 ml = _____ l

11) 10,000 ml = _____ l

12) 70, 000 ml = _____ l

Customary Capacity Measurement

✎ Convert the following measurements.

1) 78gal = _____ qt.

2) 44gal = _____ pt.

3) 75gal = _____ c.

4) 15pt. = _____ c

5) 18 qt = _____ pt.

6) 19qt = _____ c

7) 28pt. = _____ c

8) 64c = _____ gal

9) 128pt. = _____ gal

10) 112qt = _____ gal

11) 164pt. = _____ qt

12) 88c = _____ qt

13) 156c = _____ pt.

14) 192 qt = _____ gal

15) 130pt. = _____ qt

16) 86gal = _____ pt.

Metric Weight and Mass Measurement

✍ Convert.

1) 40 kg = _____ g

2) 45 kg = _____ g

3) 500 kg = _____ g

4) 50 kg = _____ g

5) 55 kg = _____ g

6) 80 kg = _____ g

7) 78 kg = _____ g

8) 62,000 g = _____ kg

9) 530,000 g = _____ kg

10) 400,000 g = _____ kg

11) 30,000 g = _____ kg

12) 20,000 g = _____ kg

13) 850,000 g = _____ kg

14) 900,000 g = _____ kg

Customary Weight and Mass Measurement

✍ Convert.

1) 6,000 lb. = _____ T

2) 12,000 lb. = _____ T

3) 8,000 lb. = _____ T

4) 14,000 lb. = _____ T

5) 32 lb. = _____ oz

6) 46 lb. = _____ oz

7) 135 lb. = _____ oz

8) 2T = _____ lb.

9) 9T = _____ lb.

10) 12T = _____ lb.

11) 15T = _____ lb.

12) 8T = _____ oz

13) 6T = _____ oz

14) 13T = _____ oz

Temperature

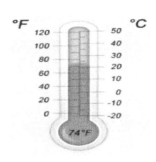

✍ Convert Fahrenheit into Celsius.

1) 14°F = ___ °C

2) 17.6°F= ___ °C

3) 23°F= ___ °C

4) 33.8°F= ___ °C

5) 68°F= ___ °C

6) 86°F= ___ °C

7) 98.6°F= ___ °C

8) 104°F= ___ °C

9) 44.6°F= ___ °C

10) 158°F= ___ °C

11) 176°F= ___ °C

12) 392°F= ___ °C

✍ Convert Celsius into Fahrenheit.

13) 0°C = ___ °F

14) 10°C = ___ °F

15) 20°C = ___ °F

16) 37°C = ___ °F

17) 50°C = ___ °F

18) 80°C = ___ °F

19) 90°C = ___ °F

20) 100°C = ___ °F

21) 2°C = ___ °F

22) 45°C = ___ °F

23) 68°C = ___ °F

24) 38°C = ___ °F

Time

✎ Convert to the units.

1) 20 hr. = _____ min

2) 14 year = _____ week

3) 7hr = _____ sec

4) 72min = _____ sec

5) 2,400min = _____ hr.

6) 1,095day = _____ year

7) 2year = _____ hr.

8) 35day = _____ hr.

9) 3 day = _____ min

10) 420min = _____ hr.

11) 20year = _____ month

12) 3,000sec = _____min

13) 216hr = _____ day

14) 15 weeks = _____ day

✎ How much time has passed?

1) From 1:15 A.M. to 4:25 A.M.: _____ hours and ___ minutes.

2) From 2:20 A.M. to 6:45 A.M.: _____ hours and ___ minutes.

3) It's 8:40 P.M. What time was 4 hours ago? _____ O'clock

4) 3:20 A.M to 6:40 AM: _____ hours and _____ minutes.

5) 2:35 A.M to 6:55 AM: _____ hours and _____ minutes.

6) 8:00 A.M. to 10:25 AM. = _____ hour(s) and _____ minutes.

7) 9:45 A.M. to 2:15 PM. = _____ hour(s) and _____ minutes

8) 9:15 A.M. to 9:50 A.M. = _____ minutes

9) 4:05 A.M. to 4:52 A.M. = _____ minutes

Money Amounts

✍ Add.

1)
$104
+$232
_____

$402
+$310
_____

$220
+$115
_____

2)
$521
+$330
_____

$330
+$401
_____

$532
+$342
_____

3)
$421
+$202
_____

$510
+$228
_____

$640
+$210
_____

4)
$521.50
+$123.70
_____

$611.20
+$320.75
_____

$415.00
+$256.30
_____

✍ Subtract.

5)
$535
−$123
_____

$441
−$130
_____

$745
−$424
_____

6)
$526
−$127
_____

$489
−$316
_____

$540
−$439
_____

7)
$446.30
−$119.50
_____

$746.50
−$228.80
_____

$742.70
−$389.50
_____

8) Linda had $13.50. She bought some game tickets for $7.15. How much did she have left?

Money: Word Problems

🖎Solve.

1) How many boxes of envelopes can you buy with $30 if one box costs $5?

2) After paying $5.12 for a salad, Ella has $41.46. How much money did she have before buying the salad?

3) How many packages of diapers can you buy with $84 if one package costs $4?

4) Last week James ran 35 miles more than Michael. James ran 68 miles. How many miles did Michael run?

5) Last Friday Jacob had $26.52. Over the weekend he received some money for cleaning the attic. He now has $45. How much money did he receive?

6) After paying $4.08 for a sandwich, Amelia has $37.50. How much money did she have before buying the sandwich?

Answers of Worksheets – Chapter 8

Metric length

1) 20 cm	6) 9 m	11) 12,000 m
2) 4,000 mm	7) 1,100 cm	12) 4,000 cm
3) 500 cm	8) 20 cm	13) 8 km
4) 6,000 m	9) 4 m	14) 9 km
5) 8 m	10) 6,000,000 mm	

Customary Length

1) 72	6) 3	11) 27
2) 36	7) 7	12) 50
3) 9	8) 5	13) 8
4) 15	9) 720	14) 180
5) 108	10) 2,088	

Metric Capacity

1) 40,000 ml	5) 27,000 ml	9) 95 ml
2) 6,000 ml	6) 13,000 ml	10) 4L
3) 40,000 ml	7) 80 ml	11) 10 L
4) 32,000 ml	8) 56 ml	12) 70 L

Customary Capacity

1) 312 qt	5) 36 pt.	9) 16 gal	13) 78 pt.
2) 352 pt.	6) 76c	10) 28 gal	14) 48 gal
3) 1,200 c	7) 56 c	11) 82 qt	15) 65 qt
4) 30 c	8) 8 gal	12) 22qt	16) 688 pt.

Metric Weight and Mass

1) 40,000 g	6) 80,000 g	11) 30 kg
2) 45,000 g	7) 78,000 g	12) 20 kg
3) 500,000 g	8) 62 kg	13) 850 kg
4) 50,000 g	9) 530 kg	14) 900 kg
5) 55,000 g	10) 400 kg	

Customary Weight and Mass

1) 3 T	6) 736 oz	11) 30,000 lb.
2) 6 T	7) 2,160 oz	12) 256,000 oz
3) 4 T	8) 4,000 lb.	13) 192,000 oz
4) 7 T	9) 18,000 lb.	14) 416,000 oz
5) 512 oz	10) 24,000 lb.	

Temperature

1) −10°C	7) 37°C	13) 32°F	19) 194°F
2) −8°C	8) 40°C	14) 50°F	20) 212°F
3) −5°C	9) 7°C	15) 68°F	21) 35.6°F
4) 1°C	10) 70°C	16) 98.6°F	22) 113°F
5) 20°C	11) 80°C	17) 122°F	23) 154.4°F
6) 30°C	12) 200°C	18) 176°F	24) 100.4°F

Time - Convert

1) 1,200 min	6) 3 year	11) 240 months
2) 728 weeks	7) 17,520hr	12) 50 min
3) 2,520 sec	8) 840 hr	13) 9 days
4) 4,320 sec	9) 4,320 min	14) 105 days
5) 40 hr	10) 7hr	

Time - Gap

1) 3:10	4) 3:20	7) 4:30
2) 4:25	5) 4:20	8) 35 minutes
3) 4:40P.M.	6) 2:25	9) 47 minutes

Add Money

1) 336, 712, 335	3) 623, 738, 850
2) 851, 731, 874	4) 645.2,931.95, 671.30

Subtract Money

5) 412–311–321	7) 326.80–517.70–353.20
6) 399–173–101	8) $6.35

Money: word problem

1) 6	3) 21	5) 18.48
2) $46.58	4) 33	6) 41.58

Chapter 9: Geometric

Topics that you'll learn in this chapter:

- ✓ Identifying Angles: Acute, Right, Obtuse, and Straight Angles

- ✓ Estimate and Measure Angles with a Protractor

- ✓ Polygon Names

- ✓ Classify Triangles

- ✓ Parallel Sides in Quadrilaterals

- ✓ Identify Parallelograms

- ✓ Identify Trapezoids

- ✓ Identify Rectangles

- ✓ Perimeter and Area of Squares

- ✓ Perimeter and Area of rectangles

- ✓ Area and Perimeter: Word Problems

- ✓ Circumference, Diameter and Radius

- ✓ Volume of Cubes and Rectangle Prisms

Identifying Angles

✍ Write the name of the angles (Acute, Right, Obtuse, and Straight).

1)

2)

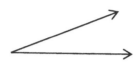

3)

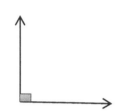

4)

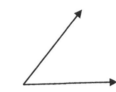

5)

6)

7)

8)

Estimate Angle Measurements

✍ Estimate the approximate measurement of each angle in degrees.

1)

2)

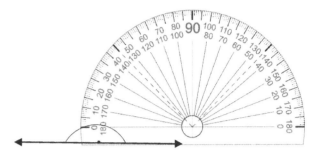

3)

4)

5)

6)

7)

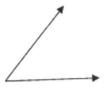

8)

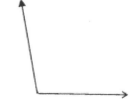

Measure Angles with a Protractor

✎ Use protractor to measure the angles below.

1)

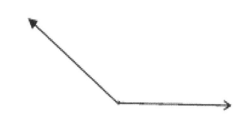

2)

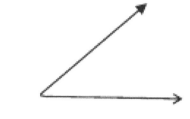

3)

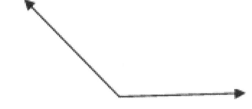

4)

✎ Use a protractor to draw angles for each measurement given.

1) 30°

2) 95°

3) 150°

4) 60

5) 45

Polygon Names

✎ Write name of polygons.

1)

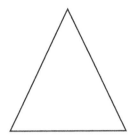

2)

3)

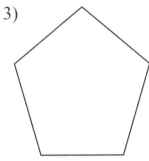

4)

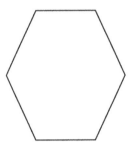

5)

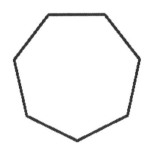

6)

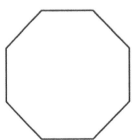

Classify Triangles

✎ Classify the triangles by their sides and angles.

1)

2)

3)

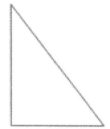

4)

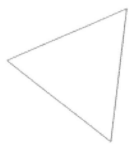

5)

6)

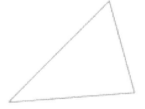

Parallel Sides in Quadrilaterals

✍ Write name of quadrilaterals.

1)

2)

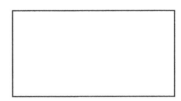

3)

4)

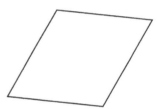

5)

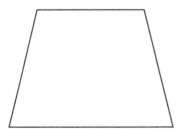

6)

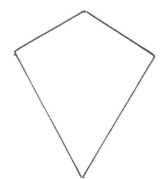

Identify Rectangles

✎Solve.

1) A rectangle has _____ sides and _____ angles.

2) Draw a rectangle that is 7centimeters long and 3 centimeters wide. What is the perimeter?

3) Draw a rectangle 4 cm long and 2 cm wide.

4) Draw a rectangle whose length is 5 cm and whose width is 3 cm. What is the perimeter of the rectangle?

5) What is the perimeter of the rectangle?

6

8

Perimeter: Find the Missing Side Lengths

✎Find the missing side of each shape.

1) perimeter = 80

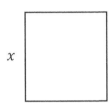

2) perimeter = 28

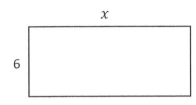

3) perimeter = 60

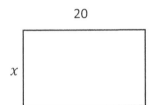

4) perimeter = 20

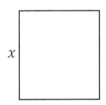

5) perimeter = 60

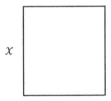

6) perimeter = 26

7) perimeter = 52

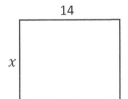

8) perimeter = 24

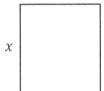

Perimeter and Area of Squares

Find perimeter and area of squares.

1) A: _____, P: _____

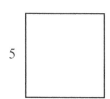

2) A: _____, P: _____

3) A: _____, P: _____

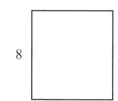

4) A: _____, P: _____

5) A: _____, P: _____

6) A: _____, P: _____

7) A: _____, P: _____

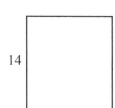

8) A: _____, P: _____

Perimeter and Area of rectangles

 Find perimeter and area of rectangles.

1) A: _____, P: _____

8
4

2) A: _____, P: _____

4
3

3) A: _____, P: _____

4
6

4) A: _____, P: _____

12
10

5) A: _____, P: _____

11
4

6) A: _____, P: _____

8
7

7) A: _____, P: _____

12.6
4

8) A: _____, P: _____

14.6
8

Find the Area or Missing Side Length of a Rectangle

 Find area or missing side length of rectangles.

1) Area =?

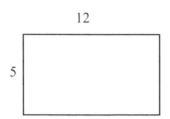

2) Area = 42, x=?

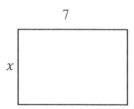

3) Area = 54, x=?

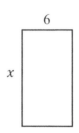

4) Area =?

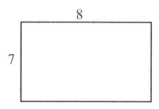

5) Area =?

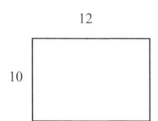

6) Area = 500, x=?

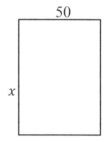

7) Area = 650, x=?

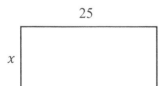

8) Area 624, x=?

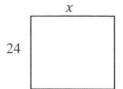

Area and Perimeter: Word Problems

✍ Solve.

1) The area of a rectangle is 96 square meters. The width is 8 meters. What is the length of the rectangle?

2) A square has an area of 64 square feet. What is the perimeter of the square?

3) Ava built a rectangular vegetable garden that is 5 feet long and has an area of 45 square feet. What is the perimeter of Ava's vegetable garden?

4) A square has a perimeter of 96 millimeters. What is the area of the square?

5) The perimeter of David's square backyard is 88 meters. What is the area of David's backyard?

6) The area of a rectangle is 32 square inches. The length is 8 inches. What is the perimeter of the rectangle?

Circumference, Diameter, and Radius

✍ Find the diameter and circumference of circles.

1)

3.75 m

2)

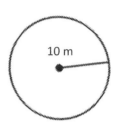

10 m

3)

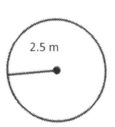

2.5 m

4)

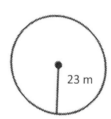

23 m

✍ Find the radius.

5)

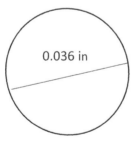

0.036 in

6)

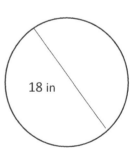

18 in

7) Diameter = 15*ft*

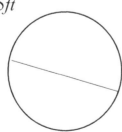

8) Diameter = 45 m

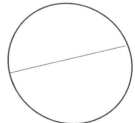

Volume of Cubes and Rectangle Prisms

✎Find the volume of each of the rectangular prisms.

1)

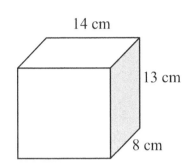

2)

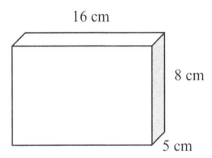

3)

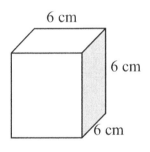

4)

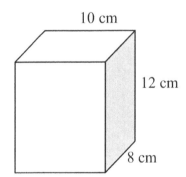

5)

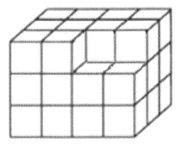

6)

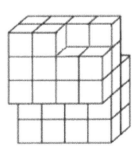

Answers of Worksheets – Chapter 9

Identifying Angles

1) Obtuse	3) Right	5) Straight	7) Obtuse
2) Acute	4) Acute	6) Obtuse	8) Acute

Estimate Angle Measurements

1) 70°	3) 20°	5) 40°	7) 50°
2) 180°	4) 80°	6) 135°	8) 100°

Measure Angles with a Protractor

1) 140∘	2) 40∘	3) 135∘	4) 160∘

Draw angles

1)

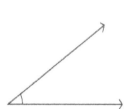

2)

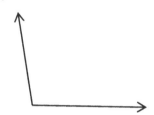

3)

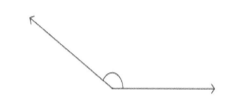

4)

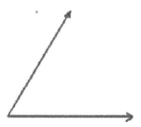

5)

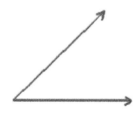

Polygon Names

1) Triangle	3) Pentagon	5) Heptagon
2) Quadrilateral	4) Hexagon	6) Octagon

Classify triangles

1) Scalene, obtuse	4) Equilateral, acute
2) Isosceles, right	5) Isosceles, acute
3) Scalene, right	6) Scalene, acute

Parallel Sides in Quadrilaterals

1) Square   3) Parallelogram   5) Trapezoid

2) Rectangle   4) Rhombus   6) Kike

Identify Rectangles

1) 4 - 4   3) Draw the square   5) 28

2) 20   4) 16

Perimeter: Find the Missing Side Lengths

1) 20   3) 10   5) 15   7) 12

2) 8   4) 5   6) 6   8) 6

Perimeter and Area of Squares

1) A: 25, P: 20   4) A: 81, P: 36   7) A: 196, P: 56

2) A: 49, P: 28   5) A: 625 P: 100   8) A: 225, P: 60

3) A: 64, P: 32   6) A: 169, P: 52

Perimeter and Area of rectangles

1) A: 32, P: 24   4) A: 120, P: 44   7) A: 50.4, P: 33.2

2) A: 12, P: 14   5) A: 44, P: 30   8) A: 116.8, P: 45.2

3) A: 24, P: 20   6) A: 56, P: 30

Find the Area or Missing Side Length of a Rectangle

1) 60   3) 9   5) 120   7) 26

2) 6   4) 56   6) 10   8) 26

Area and Perimeter: Word Problems

1) 12   3) 28   5) 484

2) 32   4) 576   6) 24

Circumference, Diameter, and Radius

1) diameter: 7.5 circumferences:7.5 π or 23.55   3) diameter: 5 circumferences: 5π or 15.7

2) diameter: 20 circumferences: 20π or 62.80   4) diameter: 46 circumferences: 46π or 144.44

5) radius: 0.018 in   6) radius: 9 in   7) radius: 7.5 ft 8) radius: 22.5 m

Volume of Cubes and Rectangle Prisms

1) 1,456 cm^3 4) 960 cm^3

2) 640 cm^3 5) 34

3) 216 c m^3 6) 42

Chapter 10: Three-Dimensional Figures

Topics that you'll learn in this chapter:

- ✓ Identify Three–Dimensional Figures

- ✓ Count Vertices, Edges, and Faces

- ✓ Identify Faces of Three–Dimensional Figures

Identify Three–Dimensional Figures

✍ Write the name of each shape.

1)

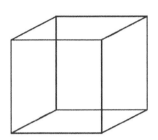

2)

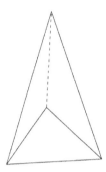

3)

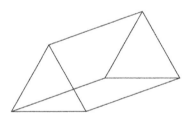

4)

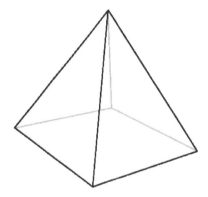

5)

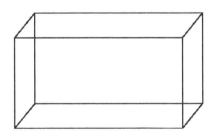

6)

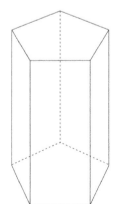

Count Vertices, Edges, and Faces

	Shape	Number of edges	Number of faces	Number of vertices
1)		_____	_____	_____
2)		_____	_____	_____
3)		_____	_____	_____
4)		_____	_____	_____
5)		_____	_____	_____
6)		_____	_____	_____

Identify Faces of Three–Dimensional Figures

✍ Write the number of faces.

1)

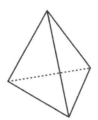

2)

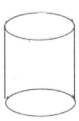

3)

4)

5)

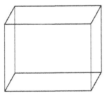

6)

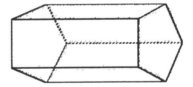

7)

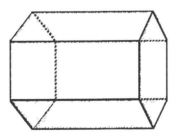

8)

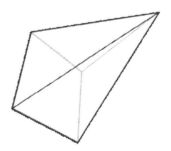

Answers of Worksheets – Chapter 10

Identify Three–Dimensional Figures

1) Cube

2) Triangular pyramid

3) Triangular prism

4) Square pyramid

5) Rectangular prism

6) Pentagonal prism

7) Hexagonal prism

Count Vertices, Edges, and Faces

Shape	Number of edges	Number of faces	Number of vertices
1)	6	4	4
2)	8	5	5
3)	12	6	8
4)	12	6	8
5)	15	7	10
6)	18	8	12

Identify Faces of Three–Dimensional Figures

1) 6

2) 2

3) 5

4) 4

5) 6

6) 7

7) 8

8) 5

Chapter 11: Symmetry and Transformations

Topics that you'll learn in this chapter:

- ✓ Line Segments

- ✓ Identify Lines of Symmetry

- ✓ Count Lines of Symmetry

- ✓ Parallel, Perpendicular and Intersecting Lines

- ✓ Translations, Rotations, and Reflections

Line Segments

✎ Write each as a line, ray or line segment.

1)

2)

3)

4)

5)

6)

7)

8)

Identify Lines of Symmetry

✍ Tell whether the line on each shape a line of symmetry is.

1)

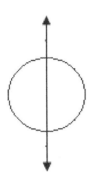

2)

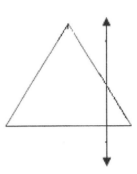

3)

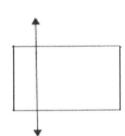

4)

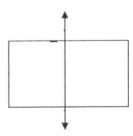

5)

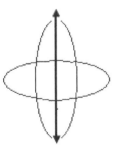

6)

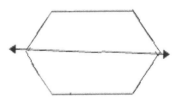

7)

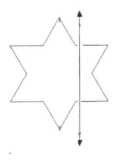

8)

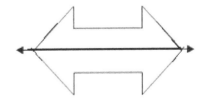

Count Lines of Symmetry

Draw lines of symmetry on each shape. Count and write the lines of symmetry you see.

1)

2)

3)

4)

5)

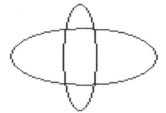

6)

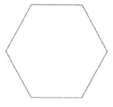

7)

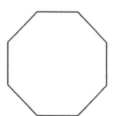

8)

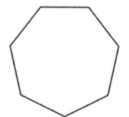

Parallel, Perpendicular and Intersecting Lines

✍ State whether the given pair of lines are parallel, perpendicular, or intersecting.

1)

2)

3)

4)

5)

6)

7)

8)

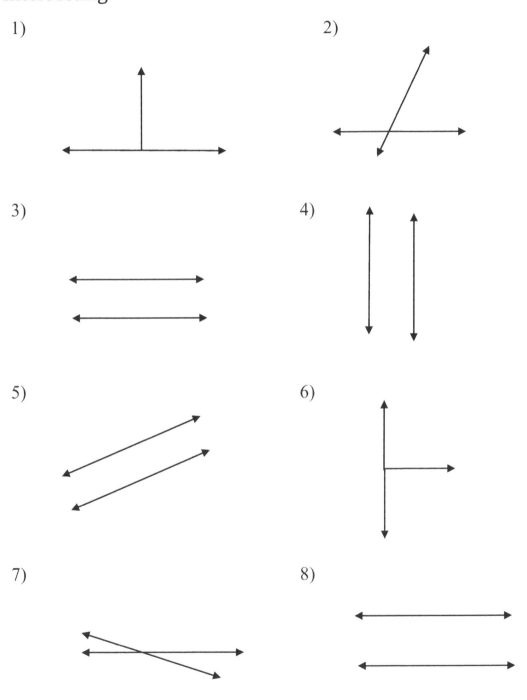

Answers of Worksheets – Chapter 11

Line Segments

1) Line segment

2) Ray

3) Line

4) Line segment

5) Ray

6) Line

7) Line

8) Line segment

Identify lines of symmetry

1) yes

2) no

3) no

4) yes

5) yes

6) yes

7) no

8) yes

Count lines of symmetry

1)

2)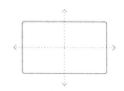

3)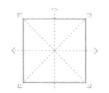

4)

5)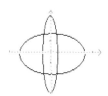

6)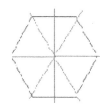

7)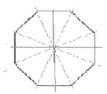

8)

Parallel, Perpendicular and Intersecting Lines

1) Perpendicular

2) Intersection

3) Parallel

4) Parallel

5) Parallel

6) Perpendicular

7) Intersection

8) Parallel

Chapter 12: Data and Graphs

Topics that you'll learn in this chapter:

- ✓ Graph Points on a Coordinate Plane

- ✓ Bar Graph

- ✓ Tally and Pictographs

- ✓ Line Graphs

- ✓ Stem–And–Leaf Plot

- ✓ Scatter Plots

Mean and Median

✎ Find Mean and Median of the Given Data.

1) $18, 16, 7, 1, 9$

2) $5, 16, 5, 17, 4, 13$

3) $13, 15, 11, 8, 19$

4) $5, 9, 1, 8, 6, 1$

5) $7, 6, 8, 5, 8, 11, 12$

6) $6, 1, 5, 5, 9, 14, 20$

7) $18, 4, 10, 5, 24, 6, 6, 21$

8) $28, 9, 2, 4, 19, 7, 22$

9) $38, 25, 41, 26, 33, 43, 61$

10) $11, 15, 1, 15, 4, 15, 8, 11$

11) $48, 16, 32, 64, 44, 33$

12) $37, 38, 58, 88, 43, 84$

13) $61, 69, 50, 57, 42, 44$

14) $96, 85, 82, 25, 71, 93, 39$

15) $98, 12, 101, 64, 37, 50$

16) $20, 77, 8, 99, 13, 46, 11$

✎ Solve.

17) In a javelin throw competition, five athletics score 76, 78, 68, 57 and 65 meters. What are their Mean and Median? _____

18) Eva went to shop and bought 13 apples, 4 peaches, 6 bananas, 2 pineapple and 5 melons. What are the Mean and Median of her purchase?

_____

Mode and Range

✎ Find Mode and Rage of the Given Data.

1) 10, 3, 5, 8, 7, 3

   Mode: _____ Range: _____

2) 7, 7, 12, 4, 17, 3, 9, 21

   Mode: _____ Range: _____

3) 2, 2, 1, 19, 8, 19, 2, 6, 2

   Mode: _____ Range: _____

4) 11, 29, 2, 29, 3, 6, 29, 7

   Mode: _____ Range: _____

5) 6, 6, 4, 6, 18, 4, 18

   Mode: _____ Range: _____

6) 0, 1, 14, 11, 8, 6, 8, 1, 5, 1

   Mode: _____ Range: _____

7) 4, 6, 2, 9, 7, 7, 6, 7, 3, 7

   Mode: _____ Range: _____

8) 9, 6, 4, 9, 6, 9, 9, 6, 3

   Mode: _____ Range: _____

9) 4, 4, 5, 8, 4, 4, 7, 8, 4, 10

   Mode: _____ Range: _____

10) 17, 9, 12, 9, 4, 9, 18, 10

   Mode: _____ Range: _____

11) 14, 1, 17, 2, 2, 12, 28, 2

   Mode: _____ Range: _____

12) 6, 18, 15, 10, 6, 6, 3, 12

   Mode: _____ Range: _____

✎ Solve.

13) A stationery sold 13 pencils, 38 red pens, 49 blue pens, 13 notebooks, 39 erasers, 44 rulers and 42 color pencils. What are the Mode and Range for the stationery sells?

   Mode: _____   Range: _____

14) In an English test, eight students score 12, 10, 18, 12, 19, 20, 16 and 11. What are their Mode and Range? _____

Graph Points on a Coordinate Plane

Plot each point on the coordinate grid.

1) A (5, 8)   3) C (2, 6)   5) E (1, 7)

2) B (4, 5)   4) D (7, 6)   6) F (8, 1)

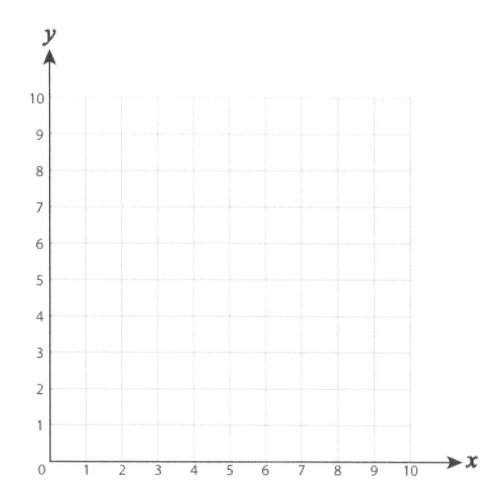

Bar Graph

Graph the given information as a bar graph.

Day	Hot dogs sold
Monday	40
Tuesday	70
Wednesday	20
Thursday	90
Friday	60

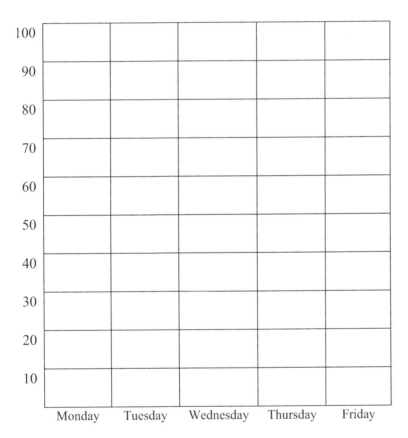

Tally and Pictographs

✎ Using the key, draw the pictograph to show the information.

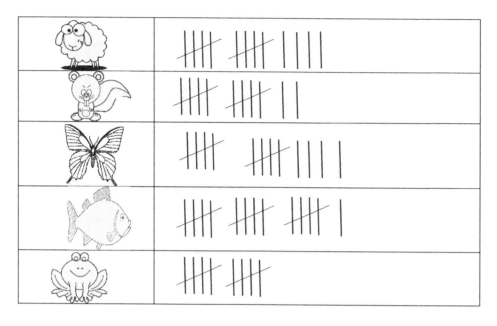

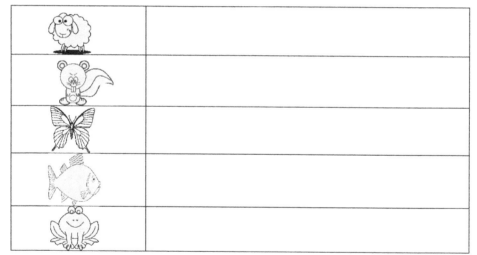

Key: = 2 animals

Line Graphs

David work as a salesman in a store. He records the number of shoes sold in five days on a line graph. Use the graph to answer the question

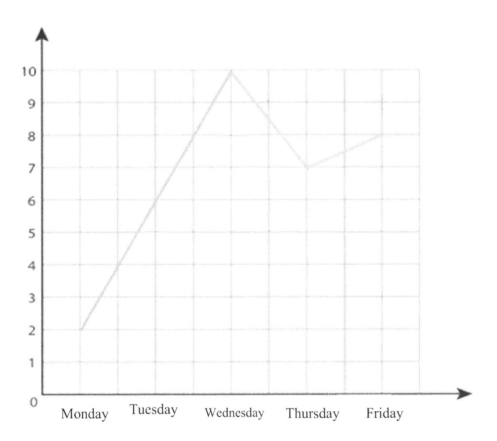

1) How many shoes were sold on Tuesday?

2) Which day had the minimum sales of shoes?

3) Which day had the maximum number of shoes sold?

4) How many shoes were sold in 5 days?

Stem–And–Leaf Plot

✎ Make stem ad leaf plots for the given data.

1) 32, 34, 37, 11, 12, 34, 58, 57, 39, 34, 18, 53

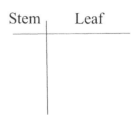

2) 21, 65, 32, 28, 25, 21, 31, 61, 69, 30, 65, 39

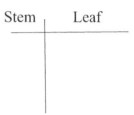

3) 122, 79, 96, 75, 100, 127, 92, 124, 78, 122, 98, 127

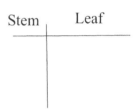

4) 64, 30, 100, 64, 72, 36, 109, 68, 75, 39, 68, 106, 70

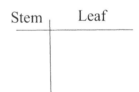

Scatter Plots

✎Construct a scatter plot.

x	1	2	3	4	5	8
y	20	30	45	60	80	10

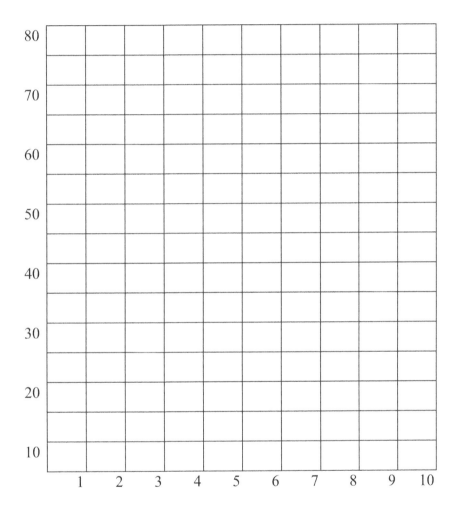

Probability Problems

✍ Solve.

1) A number is chosen at random from 1 to 10. Find the probability of selecting a 5 or smaller.

2) A number is chosen at random from 1 to 45. Find the probability of selecting multiples of 15.

3) A number is chosen at random from 1 to 10. Find the probability of selecting multiples of 2 or 3.

4) A number is chosen at random from 1 to 10. Find the probability of selecting a multiple of 4.

5) A number is chosen at random from 1 to 20. Find the probability of selecting prime numbers.

6) A number is chosen at random from 1 to 15. Find the probability of not selecting factors of 12.

Answers of Worksheets – Chapter 12

Mean and Median

1) Mean: 10.2, Median: 9

2) Mean: 10, Median: 9

3) Mean: 13.2, Median: 13

4) Mean: 5, Median: 5.5

5) Mean: 8.1, Median: 8

6) Mean: 8.57, Median: 6

7) Mean: 11.75, Median: 8

8) Mean: 13, Median: 9

9) Mean: 38.14, Median: 38

10) Mean: 10, Median: 11

11) Mean: 39.5, Median: 38.5

12) Mean: 58, Median: 50.5

13) Mean:53.83, Median: 53.5

14) Mean: 70.14, Median: 82

15) Mean: 60.33, Median: 57

16) Mean: 39.14, Median: 20

Mode and Range

1) Mode: 3, Range: 7

2) Mode: 7, Range: 18

3) Mode: 2, Range: 18

4) Mode: 29, Range: 27

5) Mode: 6, Range: 14

6) Mode: 1, Range: 14

7) Mode: 7, Range: 7

8) Mode: 9, Range6

9) Mode: 4, Range: 6

10) Mode: 11, Range: 9.5

11) Mode: 2, Range: 27

12) Mode: 6, Range: 15

13) Mode: 13, Range: 36

14) Mode: 12, Range: 10

Graph Points on a Coordinate Plane

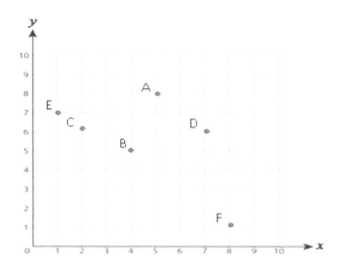

Bar Graph

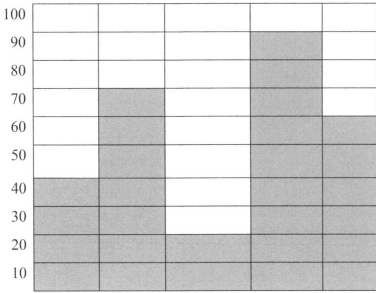

Tally and Pictographs

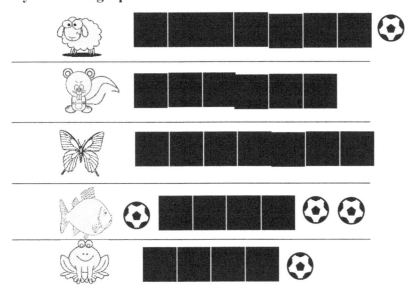

Line Graphs

1) 6   2) Monday   3) Wednesday   4) 33

Stem–And–Leaf Plot

1)

Stem	leaf
1	1 2 8
3	2 4 4 4 7 9
5	3 7 8

2)

Stem	leaf
2	1 1 5 8
3	0 1 2 9
6	1 5 5 9

3)

Stem	leaf
7	5 8 9
9	2 6 8
10	0
12	2 2 4 7 7

4)

Stem	leaf
3	0 6 9
6	4 4 8 8
7	0 2 5
10	0 6 9

Scatter Plots

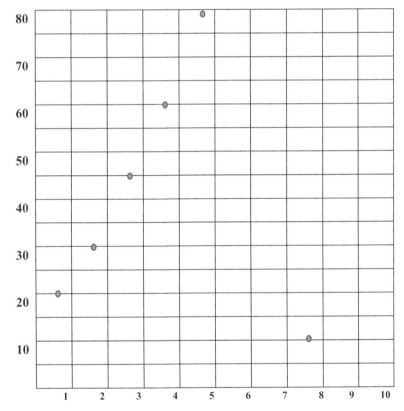

Probability Problems

1) $\frac{1}{2}$

2) $\frac{1}{15}$

3) $\frac{7}{10}$

4) $\frac{1}{5}$

5) $\frac{2}{5}$

6) $\frac{3}{5}$

ISEE Lower Level Practice Tests

The Independent School Entrance Exam (ISEE) is an admission test developed by the Educational Records Bureau for its member schools as part of their admission process.

ISEE Lower Level tests use a multiple-choice format and contain two Mathematics sections:

Quantitative Reasoning:

There are 38 questions in the Quantitative Reasoning section and students have 35 minutes to answer the questions. This section contains word problems requiring either no calculation or simple calculation.

Mathematics Achievement:

There are 30 questions in the Mathematics Achievement section and students have 30 minutes to answer the questions. Mathematics Achievement measures students' knowledge of Mathematics requiring one or more steps in calculating the answer.

In this section, there are two complete ISEE Lower Level Quantitative Reasoning and Mathematics Achievement Tests. Let your student take these tests to see what score they'll be able to receive on a real ISEE Lower Level test.

Time to Test

Time to refine your skill with a practice examination

Take a practice ISEE Lower Level Math Test to simulate the test day experience. After you've finished, score your test using the answer key.

Before You Start

- You'll need a pencil and scratch papers to take the test.

- For each question, there are four possible answers. Choose which one is best.

- It's okay to guess. You won't lose any points if you're wrong.

- Use the answer sheet provided to record your answers.

- After you've finished the test, review the answer key to see where you went wrong.

- **Calculators are NOT allowed for the ISEE Lower Level Test.**

Good Luck!

ISEE Lower Level Practice Test Answer Sheets

Remove (or photocopy) these answer sheets and use them to complete the practice tests.

ISEE Lower Level Practice Test

Quantitative Reasoning

1 Ⓐ Ⓑ Ⓒ Ⓓ	21 Ⓐ Ⓑ Ⓒ Ⓓ
2 Ⓐ Ⓑ Ⓒ Ⓓ	22 Ⓐ Ⓑ Ⓒ Ⓓ
3 Ⓐ Ⓑ Ⓒ Ⓓ	23 Ⓐ Ⓑ Ⓒ Ⓓ
4 Ⓐ Ⓑ Ⓒ Ⓓ	24 Ⓐ Ⓑ Ⓒ Ⓓ
5 Ⓐ Ⓑ Ⓒ Ⓓ	25 Ⓐ Ⓑ Ⓒ Ⓓ
6 Ⓐ Ⓑ Ⓒ Ⓓ	26 Ⓐ Ⓑ Ⓒ Ⓓ
7 Ⓐ Ⓑ Ⓒ Ⓓ	27 Ⓐ Ⓑ Ⓒ Ⓓ
8 Ⓐ Ⓑ Ⓒ Ⓓ	28 Ⓐ Ⓑ Ⓒ Ⓓ
9 Ⓐ Ⓑ Ⓒ Ⓓ	29 Ⓐ Ⓑ Ⓒ Ⓓ
10 Ⓐ Ⓑ Ⓒ Ⓓ	30 Ⓐ Ⓑ Ⓒ Ⓓ
11 Ⓐ Ⓑ Ⓒ Ⓓ	31 Ⓐ Ⓑ Ⓒ Ⓓ
12 Ⓐ Ⓑ Ⓒ Ⓓ	32 Ⓐ Ⓑ Ⓒ Ⓓ
13 Ⓐ Ⓑ Ⓒ Ⓓ	33 Ⓐ Ⓑ Ⓒ Ⓓ
14 Ⓐ Ⓑ Ⓒ Ⓓ	34 Ⓐ Ⓑ Ⓒ Ⓓ
15 Ⓐ Ⓑ Ⓒ Ⓓ	35 Ⓐ Ⓑ Ⓒ Ⓓ
16 Ⓐ Ⓑ Ⓒ Ⓓ	36 Ⓐ Ⓑ Ⓒ Ⓓ
17 Ⓐ Ⓑ Ⓒ Ⓓ	37 Ⓐ Ⓑ Ⓒ Ⓓ
18 Ⓐ Ⓑ Ⓒ Ⓓ	38 Ⓐ Ⓑ Ⓒ Ⓓ
19 Ⓐ Ⓑ Ⓒ Ⓓ	39 Ⓐ Ⓑ Ⓒ Ⓓ
20 Ⓐ Ⓑ Ⓒ Ⓓ	40 Ⓐ Ⓑ Ⓒ Ⓓ

Mathematics Achievement

1 Ⓐ Ⓑ Ⓒ Ⓓ	21 Ⓐ Ⓑ Ⓒ Ⓓ
2 Ⓐ Ⓑ Ⓒ Ⓓ	22 Ⓐ Ⓑ Ⓒ Ⓓ
3 Ⓐ Ⓑ Ⓒ Ⓓ	23 Ⓐ Ⓑ Ⓒ Ⓓ
4 Ⓐ Ⓑ Ⓒ Ⓓ	24 Ⓐ Ⓑ Ⓒ Ⓓ
5 Ⓐ Ⓑ Ⓒ Ⓓ	25 Ⓐ Ⓑ Ⓒ Ⓓ
6 Ⓐ Ⓑ Ⓒ Ⓓ	26 Ⓐ Ⓑ Ⓒ Ⓓ
7 Ⓐ Ⓑ Ⓒ Ⓓ	27 Ⓐ Ⓑ Ⓒ Ⓓ
8 Ⓐ Ⓑ Ⓒ Ⓓ	28 Ⓐ Ⓑ Ⓒ Ⓓ
9 Ⓐ Ⓑ Ⓒ Ⓓ	29 Ⓐ Ⓑ Ⓒ Ⓓ
10 Ⓐ Ⓑ Ⓒ Ⓓ	30 Ⓐ Ⓑ Ⓒ Ⓓ
11 Ⓐ Ⓑ Ⓒ Ⓓ	31 Ⓐ Ⓑ Ⓒ Ⓓ
12 Ⓐ Ⓑ Ⓒ Ⓓ	32 Ⓐ Ⓑ Ⓒ Ⓓ
13 Ⓐ Ⓑ Ⓒ Ⓓ	33 Ⓐ Ⓑ Ⓒ Ⓓ
14 Ⓐ Ⓑ Ⓒ Ⓓ	34 Ⓐ Ⓑ Ⓒ Ⓓ
15 Ⓐ Ⓑ Ⓒ Ⓓ	35 Ⓐ Ⓑ Ⓒ Ⓓ
16 Ⓐ Ⓑ Ⓒ Ⓓ	36 Ⓐ Ⓑ Ⓒ Ⓓ
17 Ⓐ Ⓑ Ⓒ Ⓓ	37 Ⓐ Ⓑ Ⓒ Ⓓ
18 Ⓐ Ⓑ Ⓒ Ⓓ	38 Ⓐ Ⓑ Ⓒ Ⓓ
19 Ⓐ Ⓑ Ⓒ Ⓓ	39 Ⓐ Ⓑ Ⓒ Ⓓ
20 Ⓐ Ⓑ Ⓒ Ⓓ	40 Ⓐ Ⓑ Ⓒ Ⓓ

ISEE Lower Level Practice Test 1

Mathematics

Quantitative Reasoning

❖ **38 Questions.**

❖ **Total time for this test: 35 Minutes.**

❖ **You may NOT use a calculator for this test.**

Administered *Month Year*

1) If 5 added to a number, the sum is 10. If the same number added to 25, the

   answer   is?

   A. 28   C. 30

   B. 34   D. 32

2) $\dfrac{4+7+6\times1+1}{4+6} = ?$

   A. $\dfrac{10}{7}$ C. $\dfrac{9}{5}$

   B. $\dfrac{5}{9}$ D. $\dfrac{8}{3}$

3) $5 \times 8 \times 12 \times 5$ is equal to the product of 40 and

   A. 5   C. 25

   B. 12   D. 60

4) If 45 can be divided by both 9 and x without leaving a remainder, then 45 can

   also be divided by which of the following?

   A. $x + 6$ C. $x - 2$

   B. $2x - 6$ D. $x \times 9$

5) Use the equations below to answer the question:

$$x + 12 = 18$$

$$16 + y = 20$$

   What is the value of $x + y$?

   A. 10   C. 8

   B. 11   D. 7

6) Which of the following expressions has the same value as $\frac{9}{2} \times \frac{8}{15}$?

A. $\frac{6 \times 3}{4}$

C. $\frac{5 \times 6}{3}$

B. $\frac{6 \times 2}{5}$

D. $\frac{3 \times 4}{5}$

7) When 5 is added to two times number N, the result is 45. Then N is ....

A. 18

C. 16

B. 20

D. 12

8) At noon, the temperature was 35 degrees. By midnight, it had dropped another 40degrees. What was the temperature at midnight?

A. 10 degrees above zero

C. 5 degrees above zero

B. 10 degrees below zero

D. 5 degrees below zero

9) If a triangle has a base of 3 cm and a height of 8 cm, what is the area of the triangle?

A. $10 \ cm^2$

C. $24 \ cm^2$

B. $12 \ cm^2$

D. $32 \ cm^2$

10) Which formula would you use to find the area of a square?

A. $length \times width \times height$

C. $length \times width$

B. $\frac{1}{2} base \times height$

D. $side \times side$

11) What is the next number in this sequence?

$$4, 8, 13, 19, 26, \ldots$$

A. 34

C. 12

B. 29

D. 35

12) What is the average of the following numbers?

$$8, 12, 14, 22, 36$$

A. 18

C. 18.4

B. 18.2

D. 22

13) If there are 4 red balls and 10 blue balls in a basket, what is the probability that John will pick out a red ball from the basket?

A. $\dfrac{14}{4}$

C. $\dfrac{2}{10}$

B. $\dfrac{2}{7}$

D. $\dfrac{3}{5}$

14) How many lines of symmetry does an equilateral triangle have?

A. 5

C. 3

B. 4

D. 2

15) What is %10 of 600?

A. 20

C. 60

B. 30

D. 6

16) Which of the following statement is False?

A. $32 \times \frac{1}{4} = 8$

C. $8 \div (2 - 1) = 1$

B. $(7 + 1) \times 5 = 40$

D. $8 \times (3 - 2) = 8$

17) If all the sides in the following figure are of equal length and length of one

side is 4, what is the perimeter of the figure?

A. 15

C. 24

B. 18

D. 32

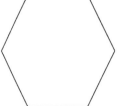

18) $\frac{4}{5} - \frac{3}{5} = ?$

A. 0.1

C. 0.2

B. 0.15

D. 0.25

19) If $N = 6$ and $\frac{36}{N} + 4 = \Box$, then $\Box = \dots.$

A. 10

C. 12

B. 14

D. 10

20) Three people can paint 3 houses in 12 days. How many people are needed to

paint 6 houses in 6 days?

A. 6

C. 12

B. 8

D. 16

21) Which of the following is greater than $\frac{18}{27}$?

A. $\frac{1}{4}$ C. $\frac{1}{3}$

B. $\frac{5}{2}$ D. 0.24

The result of a research shows the number of men and women in four cities of a country.

Number of men and women in four cities

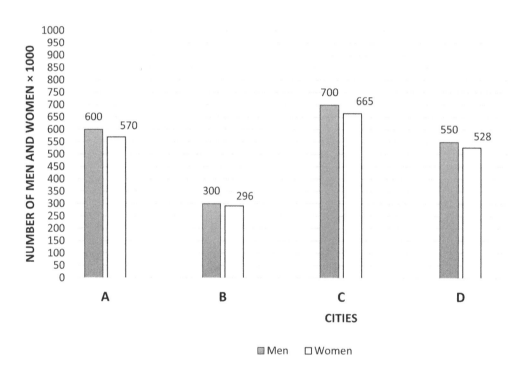

22) What is the difference of the population of men in the biggest city and in the smallest city?

A. 341   C. 400

B. 451   D. 240

23) 8.9 − 5.08 is closest to which of the following.

    A. 3.7   C. 3.6

    B. 3.8   D. 4.2

24) Numbers x and y are shown below. How many times larger is the value of digit 4 in the number x, than the value of digit 6 in the number y?

$$x = 3{,}843 \quad y = 345$$

    A. 10   C. 100

    B. 1   D. 1,000

25) What is 3,489.76853 rounded to the nearest tenth?

    A. 3,489.768   C. 3,489

    B. 3,489.8   D. 3,489.77

26) $6a + 18 = 48, a = ?$

    A. 5   C. 8

    B. 3   D. 10

27) Two angles of a triangle measure 45 and 65. What is the measure of third angle?

    A. 65   C. 95

    B. 105   D. 70

28) A woman weighs 146 pounds. She gains 26 pounds one month and 10 pounds the next month. What is her new weight?

A. 182 Pounds

C. 182 Pounds

B. 158 Pounds

D. 152 Pounds

29) If $\frac{1}{5}$ of a number is greater than 6, the number must be ……

A. Less than 5

C. Equal to 30

B. Equal to 20

D. Greater than 30

30) If $7 \times (M + N) = 63$ and M is greater than 0, then N could Not be ……

A. 1

C. 4

B. 7

D. 9

31) At a Zoo, the ratio of lions to tigers is 24 to 16. Which of the following could NOT be the total number of lions and tigers in the zoo?

A. 20

C. 76

B. 40

D. 35

32) In the multiplication bellow, A represents which digit?

$$14 \times 5A2 = 7,868$$

A. 3

C. 6

B. 4

D. 9

33) If N is an even number, which of the following is always an odd number?

A. $\frac{N}{2}$

C. $2N$

B. $N + 4$

D. $N + 1$

34) In a basket, there are equal numbers of red, white, yellow, and purple cards. Which of the following could be the number of cards in the basket?

A. 82   C. 30

B. 122   D. 44

35) Jim types 120 words per minute. How many words does he type in 15 seconds?

A. 18   C. 26

B. 16   D. 30

36) Which of the following is NOT equal to $\frac{4}{9}$?

A. $\frac{44}{99}$ C. $\frac{32}{72}$

B. $\frac{28}{63}$ D. $\frac{16}{45}$

37) Which of the following is closest to 8.03?

A. 7   C. 8

B. 8.5   D. 8.4

38) What is the median of these numbers? 7, 9, 13, 11, 20, 22, 6

A. 22   C. 11

B. 13   D. 9

STOP

IF YOU FINISH BEFORE TIME IS CALLED, YOU MAY CHECK YOUR WORK ON THIS SECTION ONLY. DO NOT TURN TO ANY OTHER SECTION IN THE TEST.

ISEE Lower Level Practice Test 1

Mathematics

Mathematics Achievement

- ❖ 30 Questions.
- ❖ Total time for this test: 30 Minutes.
- ❖ You may NOT use a calculator for this test.

Administered *Month Year*

1) What is 6,563.3752 rounded to the nearest tenth?

A. 6,563.4

C. 6,563

B. 6,563.375

D. 6,563.37

2) Which of the following fractions is the largest?

A. $\frac{4}{7}$

C. $\frac{5}{7}$

B. $\frac{1}{5}$

D. $\frac{2}{7}$

3) A bag contains 20 balls: two green, five black, eight blue, a brown, a red and one white. If 18 balls are removed from the bag at random, what is the probability that a brown ball has been removed?

A. $\frac{1}{10}$

C. $\frac{2}{18}$

B. $\frac{9}{20}$

D. $\frac{9}{10}$

4) From last year, the price of gasoline has increased from $1.45 per gallon to $2.03 per gallon. The new price is what percent of the original price?

A. 85%

C. 120%

B. 140%

D. 130%

5) Emma purchased a computer for $423.80. The computer is regularly priced at $652. What was the percent discount Emma received on the computer?

A. 15%

C. 25%

B. 45%

D. 35%

6) In the given diagram, the height is 10 cm. what is the area of the triangle?

A. 64 cm²

B. 96 cm²

C. 180 cm²

D. 356 cm²

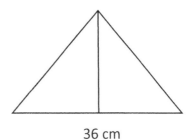

36 cm

7) Two angles of a triangle measure 39 and 45. What is the measure of the third angle?

A. 96   C. 105

B. 40   D. 35

8) $\frac{1}{5} + \frac{3}{4} =$

A. $\frac{4}{9}$ C. $\frac{3}{4}$

B. $\frac{3}{9}$ D. $\frac{19}{20}$

9) What's the least common multiple (LCM) of 7 and 15?

A. have no common multiples   C. 85

B. 125   D. 120

10) While at work, Emma checks her email once every 80 minutes. In 8-hour, how many times does she check her email?

A. 9 Times   C. 10 Times

B. 4 Times   D. 6 Times

Use the following table to answer question below.

DANIEL'S BIRD-WATCHING PROJECT

DAY	NUMBER OF RAPTORS SEEN
Monday	?
Tuesday	12
Wednesday	15
Thursday	10
Friday	3
MEAN	10

11) This table shows the data Daniel collects while watching birds for one week.

How many raptors did Daniel see on Monday?

A. 10   C. 14

B. 9   D. 12

12) Which of the following is NOT a factor of 32?

A. 8   C. 10

B. 2   D. 16

13) If a rectangular swimming pool has a perimeter of 84 feet and is 11 feet wide,

what is its area?

A. 341   C. 190

B. 696   D. 146

14) Which of the following is an obtuse angle?

A. 150°

C. 76°

B. 80°

D. 45°

15) In the following figure, the shaded squares are what fractional part of the whole set of squares?

A. $\frac{1}{2}$

B. $\frac{5}{8}$

C. $\frac{2}{3}$

D. $\frac{3}{5}$

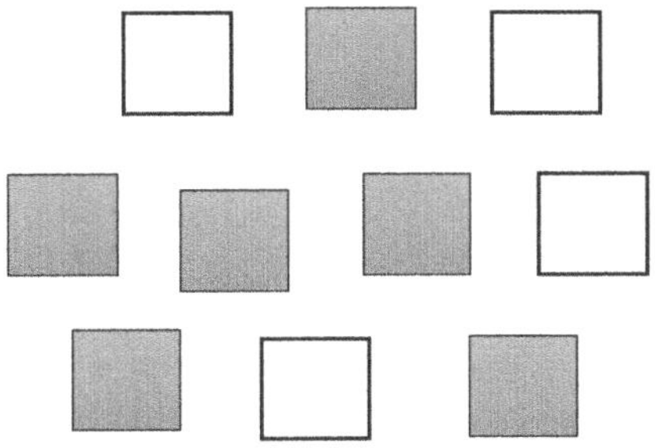

16) If a box contains red and blue balls in ratio of 2: 3 red to blue, how many red balls are there if 60 blue balls are in the box?

A. 22

C. 33

B. 40

D. 18

17) A shirt costing $300 is discounted 35%. After a month, the shirt is discounted another 25%. Which of the following expressions can be used to find the selling price of the shirt?

A. $(300)(0.70)$

B. $(300) - 300(0.30)$

C. $(300)(0.15) - (300)(0.15)$

D. $(300)(0.65)(0.75)$

18) Emma draws a shape on her paper. The shape has four sides. It has only one pair of parallel sides. What shape does Emma draw?

A. Parallelogram

C. Square

B. Rectangle

D. Trapezoid

19) If $A = 40$, then which of the following equations are correct?

A. $A + 40 = 80 - A$

C. $40 \times A = 120 \div A$

B. $A \div 40 = 80 \times A$

D. $A - 40 = 80 + A$

20) Joe makes $2.25 per hour at his work. If he works 8 hours, how much money will he earn?

A. $18.5

C. $18

B. $19

D. $18.25

21) In a classroom of 72 students, 42 are male. About what percentage of the class is female?

A. 55%

C. 59%

B. 54%

D. 53%

22) Nancy ordered 16 pizzas. Each pizza has 8 slices. How many slices of pizza did Nancy ordered?

A. 120

C. 140

B. 128

D. 160

23) Mike is 9.5 miles ahead of Julia running at 5.5 miles per hour and Julia is running at the speed of 6 miles per hour. How long does it take Julia to catch Mike?

A. 5 hours   C. 9.5 hours

B. 4.5 hours   D. 19 hours

24) Convert 0.045 to a percent.

A. 0.04%   C. 4.50%

B. 0.45%   D. 45%

25) Julie gives 3 pieces of candy to each of her friends. If Julie gives all her candy away, which amount of candy could have been the amount she distributed?

A. 97   C. 356

B. 156   D. 223

26) A taxi driver earns $6 per 1-hour work. If he works 10 hours a day and in 1 hour, he uses 4-liters petrol with price $1 for 1-liter. How much money does he earn in one day?

A. $20   C. $50

B. $48   D. $70

27) The number 0.04 can also represented by which of the following?

A. $\frac{4}{10}$ C. $\frac{4}{1,000}$

B. $\frac{4}{100}$ D. $\frac{4}{10,000}$

28)
$$\begin{array}{r} 35 \text{ hr. } 10 \text{ min.} \\ - 23 \text{ hr. } 38 \text{ min.} \\ \hline \end{array}$$

A. 12 hr. 18 min.

C. 11 hr. 32 min.

B. 12 hr. 42 min.

D. 11 hr. 57 min.

29) 180 students took an exam and 30 of them failed. What percent of the students passed the exam?

A. 15 %

C. 42 %

B. 25 %

D. 63 %

30) The width of a box is one third of its length. The height of the box is one third of its width. If the length of the box is 18 cm, what is the volume of the box?

A. 98 cm^3

C. 243 cm^3

B. 365 cm^3

D. 486 cm^3

STOP

IF YOU FINISH BEFORE TIME IS CALLED, YOU MAY CHECK YOUR WORK ON THIS SECTION ONLY. DO NOT TURN TO ANY OTHER SECTION IN THE TEST.

ISEE Lower Level Practice Test 2

Mathematics

Quantitative Reasoning

❖ **38 Questions.**

❖ **Total time for this test: 35 Minutes**.

❖ **You may NOT use a calculator for this test.**

Administered *Month Year*

1) Find the missing number in the sequence: 6, 9, 13, ..., 24

   A. 12   C. 15

   B. 24   D. 18

2) The length of a rectangle is 4 times of its width. If the length is 12, what is the perimeter of the rectangle?

   A. 22   C. 30

   B. 18   D. 42

3) Mary has y dollars. John has $10 more than Mary. If John gives Mary $16, then in terms of y, how much does John have now?

   A. $y + 4$ C. $y - 6$

   B. $y + 8$ D. $y - 3$

4) Dividing 106 by 8 leaves a remainder of

   A. 1   C. 3

   B. 5   D. 2

5) If $7,000 + A - 400 = 8,700$, then $A =$

   A. 200   C. 2,000

   B. 600   D. 2,200

6) When 79 is divided by 6, the remainder is the same as when 37 is divided by?

   A. 2   C. 5

   B. 4   D. 1

7) For what price is 35 percent off the same as $105 off?

    A. $300   C. $150

    B. $200   D. $450

8) Which of the following fractions is less than $\frac{5}{2}$?

    A. 1.7   C. 3

    B. $\frac{7}{2}$ D. 2.8

9) Use the equation below to answer the question.

$$x + 3 = 7$$

$$6y = 36$$

What is the value of $y - x$?

    A. 1   C. 3

    B. 5   D. 2

10) If $362 - x + 112 = 280$, then $x = $?

    A. 101   C. 194

    B. 156   D. 223

11) In the following right triangle, what is the value of x?

    A. 15

    B. 30

    C. 45

    D. 60

12 cm

12 cm

$x°$

12) Of the following, 15 percent of $32.99 is closest to

    A.$12.00   C.$7.00

    B.$10.00   D.$18.00

13) Solve: $11.08 - 6.6 = $ ....?

    A.2.42   C.4.48

    B.2.46   D.4.6

14) $\frac{5}{2} - \frac{3}{2} = ?$

    A.1   C.2.2

    B.1.5   D.2.4

15) When 5 is added to two times a number N, the result is 25. Which of the following equations represents this statement?

    A.$2 + 5N = 25$ C.$2N + 5 = 25$

    B.$25N + 2 = 5$ D.$2N + 25 = 5$

16) If $48 = 2 \times N + 16$, then $N = $ ....

    A.13   C.10

    B.16   D.14

17) John has 3,400 cards and Max has 625 cards. How many more cards does John have than Max?

    A.2,775   C.1,412

    B.2,065   D.1,986

18) What is 4 percent of 650?

    A. 38

    B. 26

    C. 30

    D. 36

19) Which of the following statements is False?

    A. $(5 \times 2 + 12) \times 3 = 66$

    B. $(2 \times 5 + 8) \div 2 = 9$

    C. $4 + (4 \times 6) = 28$

    D. $32 \div (3 + 5) = 5$

20) The distance between cities A and B is approximately 2,600 miles. If Nicole drives an average of 68 miles per hour, how many hours will it take her to drive from city A to city B?

    A. approximately 29 hours

    B. approximately 16 hours

    C. approximately 30 hours

    D. approximately 38 hours

21) $\frac{12}{25}$ is equal to:

    A. 4.2

    B. 0.22

    C. 0.48

    D. 0.23

22) Which of the following is NOT a prime factor of 90?

    A. 2

    B. 3

    C. 5

    D. 9

23) A writer finishes 140 pages of his manuscript in 20 hours. How many pages is his average?

    A. 16

    B. 7

    C. 18

    D. 8

Number of clothes sold in a clothing store

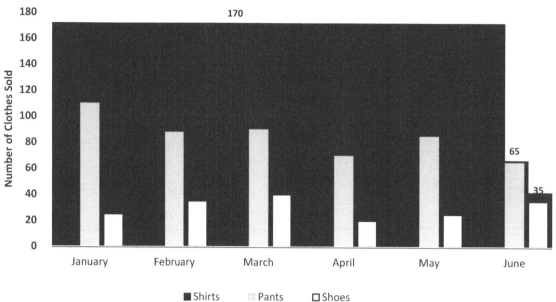

24) During the six-month period shown, what is the median number of pants per month?

A. 80

C. 85

B. 86.5

D. 88

25) A trash container, when empty, weighs 35 pounds. If this container is filled with a load of trash that weighs 350 pounds, what is the total weight of the container and its contents?

A. 245 pounds

C. 260 pounds

B. 385 pounds

D. 165 pounds

26) $14a + 20 = 160, a = ?$

A. 10

C. 14

B. 20

D. 18

27) What is the place value of 4 in 8.6345?

    A. Hundredths   C. Ten thousandths

    B. Thousandths   D. Hundred thousandths

28) Which of these numbers is equal to $\frac{55}{1,000}$?

    A. 5.5   C. 0.055

    B. 0.55   D. 0.0055

29) During a 21-hour day, Moe works $\frac{1}{3}$ of the time. How many hours does Moe work in that day?

    A. 10   C. 7

    B. 8   D. 5

30) In a basket, the ratio of red marbles to blue marbles is 6 to 2. Which of the following could NOT be the total number of red and blue marbles in the basket?

    A. 24   C. 35

    B. 32   D. 72

31) A square has an area of $81\,cm^2$. What is its perimeter?

    A. $28\,cm^2$ C. $30\,cm^2$

    B. $36\,cm^2$ D. $32\,cm^2$

32) If $300 + \square - 180 = 1,200$, then $\square = ?$

    A. 950   C. 1,102

    B. 1,050   D. 1,080

33) There are 80 students in a class. If the ratio of the number of girls to the total number of students in the class is $\frac{1}{4}$, which are the following is the number of boys in that class?

    A. 20   C. 45

    B. 30   D. 35

34) If $N \times (7 - 5) = 32$ then $N =$?

    A. 16   C. 13

    B. 10   D. 12

35) If $x \blacksquare y = 4x + y - 5$, what is the value of $2 \blacksquare 10$?

    A. 24   C. 15

    B. 13   D. 30

36) Of the following, which number if the greatest?

    A. 0.059   C. 0.5923

    B. 0.5921   D. 0.4499

37) $\frac{7}{8} - \frac{3}{4} = ?$

    A. 0.125   C. 0.5

    B. 0.126   D. 0.625

38) Which of the following is the closest to 3.03?

    A. 3.3   C. 3.4

    B. 3   D. 3.5

7) Lily and Ella are in a pancake–eating contest. Lily can eat four pancakes per minute, while Ella can eat $2\frac{1}{2}$ pancakes per minute. How many total pancakes can they eat in 3 minutes?

A. 16.5 Pancakes

B. 35.5 Pancakes

C. 19.5 Pancakes

D. 18.5 Pancakes

8) $0.82 + 1.5 + 3.23 = ?$

A. 4.5

B. 3.4

C. 5.55

D. 6.3

9) What is the perimeter of a rectangle that has a length of 8 inches and a width of 5 inches?

A. 15

B. 26

C. 32

D. 24

10) How many $\frac{1}{9}$ cup servings are in a package of cheese that contains $6\frac{1}{3}$ cups altogether?

A. 18

B. 32

C. 26

D. 57

11) Which expression is equal to $\frac{7}{11}$?

A. $7 - 11$

B. $7 \div 11$

C. 7×11

D. $\frac{11}{7}$

STOP

IF YOU FINISH BEFORE TIME IS CALLED, YOU MAY CHECK YOUR WORK ON THIS SECTION ONLY. DO NOT TURN TO ANY OTHER SECTION IN THE TEST.

ISEE Lower Level Practice Test 2

Mathematics

Mathematics Achievement

- ❖ **30 Questions.**
- ❖ **Total time for this test: 30 Minutes.**
- ❖ **You may NOT use a calculator for this test.**

Administered *Month Year*

1) What's the greatest common factor of the 16 and 32?

   A. 4

           C. 16

   B. 9

           D. 8

2) Which is sixty-two thousand, five hundred nineteen?

   A. 62,519

           C. 602,519

   B. 620,519

           D. 655,019

3) What is the name of a rectangle with sides of equal length?

   A. Hexagon

           C. Pentagon

   B. Octagon

           D. Square

4) With what number must 3.657313 be multiplied in order to obtain the number 36,573.13?

   A. 100

           C. 10,000

   B. 1,000

           D. 100,000

5) A right triangle has two short sides with lengths 8 and 6. What is the perimeter of the triangle?

   A. 7

           C. 14

   B. 24

           D. 15

6) Which expression has a value of -20?

   A. $5 - (-2) + (-27)$

           C. $-6 \times (-4) + (-2) \times (-7)$

   B. $-5 + (-5) \times (-4)$

           D. $(-2) \times (-15) + 20$

12) If the following clock shows a time in the morning, what time was it 5 hours and 30 minutes ago?

A. 08:45 AM

B. 06:45 AM

C. 08:45 PM

D. 06:45 PM

13) Which of the following is not a multiple of 6?

A. 14   C. 36

B. 18   D. 30

14) The area of a rectangle is 84 square meters. The width is 4 meters. What is the length of the rectangle?

A. 16   C. 21

B. 12   D. 18

15) The temperature on Sunday at 12:00 PM was 76°F. Low temperature on the same day was 44°F cooler. Which temperature is closest to the low temperature on that day?

A. 76°F   C. 38°F

B. 32°F   D. 85°

16) $(8^2 - 4^2) \div (4^2 \div 2) = $ __

A. $\frac{4}{3}$ C. 5

B. 6   D. $\frac{5}{4}$

Use the table below to answer the question.

City Populations	
City	**Population**
Denton	28,069
Bomberg	29,521
Windham	29,562
Sanhill	27,760

17) Which list of city populations is in order from least to greatest?

A. 28,069; 29,521; 29,562; 27,760

B. 29,562; 29,521; 28,069; 27,760

C. 27,760; 28,069; 29,521; 29,562

D. 27,760; 29,521; 28,069; 29,562

18) Ella buys five items costing $3.23, $13.65, $2.50, $4.66, and $10.34. What is the estimated total cost of Ella's items?

A. between $15 and $20   C. between $32 and $38

B. between $25 and $30   D. between $20 and $25

19) How long is the line segment shown on the number line below?

A. 6   C. 10

B. 7   D. 8

20) Which fraction has the least value?

A. $\frac{3}{2}$　　　　　　　　　　C. $\frac{5}{4}$

B. $\frac{4}{8}$　　　　　　　　　　D. $\frac{7}{16}$

21) What fraction of each shape is shaded?

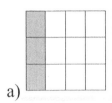 a)　　　　　　　　b)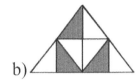

A. a. $\frac{3}{9}$; b. $\frac{3}{5}$　　　　　　C. a. $\frac{1}{4}$; b. $\frac{3}{8}$

B. a. $\frac{3}{8}$; b. $\frac{3}{12}$　　　　　D. a. $\frac{9}{12}$; b. $\frac{5}{8}$

22) Which statement about the number 897,357.16 is true?

A. The digit 6 has a value of (6×100)

B. The digit 7 has a value of (7×100)

C. The digit 5 has a value of (5×10)

D. The digit 1 has a value of (1×10)

23) Elise described a number using these clues:

Three – digit odd numbers that have a 6 in the hundreds place and a 3 in the

tens place

Which number could fit Elise's description?

A. 673　　　　　　　　　　C. 632

B. 637　　　　　　　　　　D. 623

24) Jason's favorite sports team has won 0.58 of its games this season. How can Jason express this decimal as a fraction?

A. $\frac{5}{6}$

C. $\frac{29}{25}$

B. $\frac{100}{58}$

D. $\frac{29}{100}$

25) The following graph shows the mark of six students in mathematics. What is the mean (average) of the marks?

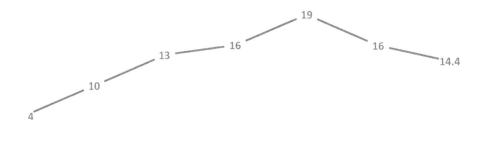

A. 13

C. 13.5

B. 13.2

D. 14

26) In the deck of cards, there are 5 spades, 6 hearts, 8 clubs, and 10 diamonds. What is the probability that William will pick out a spade?

A. $\frac{5}{29}$

C. $\frac{1}{9}$

B. $\frac{1}{23}$

D. $\frac{1}{29}$

27) There are 65 students from Riddle Elementary school at the library on Monday. The other 16 students in the school are practicing in the classroom. Which number sentence shows the total number of students in Riddle Elementary school?

A. $65 + 16$ C. 65×16

B. $65 - 16$ D. $65 \div 16$

28) There are 365 days in a year, and 24 hours in a day. How many hours are in a year?

A. 3,120   C. 4,679

B. 6,460   D. 8,760

29) $\frac{17}{21}$ is equal to:

A. 0.81   C. 34.89

B. 8.79   D. 365.00

30) Which number correctly completes the number sentence $30 \times 12 = ?$

A. 560   C. 1,100

B. 860   D. 360

STOP

IF YOU FINISH BEFORE TIME IS CALLED, YOU MAY CHECK YOUR WORK ON THIS SECTION ONLY. DO NOT TURN TO ANY OTHER SECTION IN THE TEST.

Answers and Explanations

ISEE Lower Level Practice Tests

Answer Key

❊ Now, it's time to review your results to see where you went wrong and what areas you need to improve!

ISEE Lower Level Practice Test 1 - Mathematics

Quantitative Reasoning								Mathematics Achievement				
1	C	16	C	31	C		1	A	16	B
2	C	17	C	32	C		2	C	17	D
3	D	18	C	33	D		3	D	18	D
4	D	19	D	34	D		4	B	19	A
5	A	20	C	35	D		5	D	20	C
6	D	21	B	36	D		6	C	21	A
7	B	22	C	37	C		7	A	22	B
8	D	23	B	38	C		8	D	23	D
9	B	24	A				9	D	24	C
10	D	25	B				10	D	25	B
11	A	26	A				11	A	26	A
12	C	27	D				12	C	27	B
13	B	28	C				13	A	28	C
14	C	29	D				14	A	29	D
15	C	30	D				15	D	30	D

Answers and Explanations

ISEE Lower Level Practice Tests

ISEE Lower Level Practice Test 2 - Mathematics									
Quantitative Reasoning						**Mathematics Achievement**			
1	B	16	B	31	B	1	C	16	B
2	C	17	A	32	D	2	A	17	C
3	C	18	B	33	C	3	D	18	C
4	D	19	D	34	A	4	C	19	B
5	C	20	D	35	B	5	B	20	D
6	D	21	C	36	C	6	A	21	C
7	A	22	D	37	A	7	C	22	C
8	A	23	B	38	B	8	C	23	B
9	D	24	B			9	B	24	C
10	C	25	B			10	D	25	B
11	C	26	A			11	B	26	A
12	D	27	B			12	C	27	A
13	C	28	C			13	A	28	D
14	A	29	C			14	C	29	A
15	C	30	C			15	B	30	D

Score Your Test

ISEE Lower Level scores are broken down by four sections: Verbal Reasoning, Reading Comprehension, Quantitative Reasoning, and Mathematics Achievement. A sum of the ALL sections is also reported. The Essay section is scored separately. For the Lower Level ISEE, the score range is 760 to 940, the lowest possible score a student can earn is 760 and the highest score is 940 for each section. A student receives 1 point for every correct answer. There is no penalty for wrong or skipped questions.

The total scaled score for a Lower Level ISEE test is the sum of the scores for all sections. A student will also receive a percentile score of between 1-99% that compares that student's test scores with those of other test takers of same grade and gender from the past 3 years. When a student receives her/his score, the percentile score is also be broken down into a stanine and the stanines are ranging from 1–9. Most schools accept students with scores of 5–9. The ideal candidate has scores of 6 or higher.

The following charts provide an estimate of students ISEE Lower Level percentile rankings for the practice tests, compared against other students taking these tests. Keep in mind that these percentiles are estimates only, and your actual ISEE Lower Level percentile will depend on the specific group of students taking the exam in your year.

Percentile Rank	Stanine
1 – 3	1
4 – 10	2
11- 22	3
23 – 39	4
40 – 59	5
60 – 76	6
77- 88	7
89 – 95	8
96 – 99	9

ISEE Lower Level Quantitative Reasoning Percentiles			
Grade Applying to	**25th Percentile**	**50th Percentile**	**75th Percentile**
Grade 5	825	840	860
Grade 6	838	855	870

ISEE Lower Level Mathematics Achievement Percentiles			
Grade Applying to	**25th Percentile**	**50th Percentile**	**75th Percentile**
Grade 5	830	850	865
Grade 6	855	865	978

Use the next table to convert ISEE Lower level raw score to scaled score for application to grade 5 and grade 6.

ISEE Lower Level Scaled Scores

Raw Score	Quantitative Reasoning		Mathematics Achievement		Raw Score	Quantitative Reasoning		Mathematics Achievement	
	Grade 5	Grade 6	Grade 5	Grade 6		Grade 5	Grade 6	Grade 5	Grade 6
0	760	760	760	760	26	900	885	900	890
1	770	765	770	765	27	905	890	910	900
2	780	770	780	770	28	910	895	925	920
3	790	775	790	775	29	910	900	935	930
4	800	780	800	780	30	915	905	940	940
5	810	785	810	785	31	920	910		
6	820	790	820	790	32	925	915		
7	825	795	825	795	33	930	920		
8	830	800	830	800	34	930	925		
9	835	805	835	805	35	930	925		
10	840	810	840	810	36	935	930		
11	845	815	845	815	37	935	935		
12	850	820	850	820	38	940	940		
13	855	825	855	825					
14	860	830	855	830					
15	865	835	860	835					
16	870	840	860	840					
17	875	845	865	840					
18	880	845	865	845					
19	880	850	870	845					
20	885	855	870	850					
21	885	860	875	850					
22	890	865	875	855					
23	890	870	875	855					
24	895	875	880	860					
25	895	880	890	880					

Answers and Explanations

ISEE - Lower Level

Practice Tests 1: Quantitative Reasoning

1) Answer: C.

Let x be the number. Then:

$5 + x = 10 \rightarrow x = 5 \rightarrow 5 + 25 = 30$

2) Answer: C.

$\frac{4+7+6\times1+1}{4+6} = \frac{18}{10} = \frac{9}{5}$

3) Answer: D.

$5 \times 8 \times 12 \times 5$ is equal to the product of 40 and 60.

$(5 \times 8) \times (12 \times 5) = 40 \times 60$

4) Answer: D.

$45 = x \times 9 \rightarrow x = 45 \div 9 = 5$

x equals to 5. Let's review the options provided:

A) $x + 6 \rightarrow 5 + 6 = 11$ 45 is not divisible by 11.

B) $2x - 6 \rightarrow 2 \times 5 - 6 = 4$ 45 is not divisible by 4.

C) $x - 2 \rightarrow 5 - 2 = 3$ 45 is not divisible by 3.

D) $x \times 9 \rightarrow 5 \times 9 = 45$ 45 is divisible by 45.

The answer is D.

5) Answer: A.

$x + 12 = 18 \rightarrow x = 6$

$16 + y = 20 \rightarrow y = 4$

$x + y = 6 + 4 = 10$

6) Answer: D.

$\frac{9}{2} \times \frac{8}{15} = \frac{72}{30} = \frac{24}{10}$

Choice D is equal to $\frac{12}{5} \cdot \frac{3\times4}{5} = \frac{12}{5}$

7) Answer: B.

$$5 + 2N = 45 \rightarrow 2N = 45 - 5 = 40 \rightarrow N = 20$$

8) Answer: D.

$$35 - 40 = -5$$

The temperature at midnight was 5 degrees below zero.

9) Answer: B.

Area of a triangle $= \frac{1}{2} \times (base) \times (height) = \frac{1}{2} \times 3 \times 8 = 12$

10) Answer: D.

$area\ of\ a\ square = side \times side$

Side

11) Answer: A.

First, find the pattern,

$$4 + 4 = 8 \rightarrow 8 + 5 = 13 \rightarrow 13 + 6 = 19 \rightarrow 19 + 7 = 26$$

The difference of two consecutive numbers increase by 1. The difference of 19 and 26 is 7. So, the next number should be 34. $26 + 8 = 34$

12) Answer: C.

average$= \frac{sum\ of\ all\ numbers}{number\ of\ numbers} = \frac{8+12+14+22+36}{5} = 18.4$

13) Answer: B.

There are 4 red ball and 10 are total number of balls.

Therefore, probability that John will pick out a red ball from the basket is 4 out of 14 or $\frac{4}{4+10} = \frac{4}{14} = \frac{2}{7}$.

14) Answer: C.

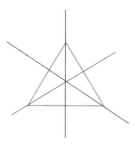

An equilateral triangle has 3 lines of symmetry.

15) Answer: C.

10 percent of $600 = 10\%$ of $600 = \frac{10}{100} \times 600 = 60$

16) Answer: C.

Let's review the options provided:

A. $32 \times \frac{1}{4} = \frac{32}{4} = 8$		This is true!
B. $(7 + 1) \times 5 = 40$		This is true!
C. $8 \div (2 - 1) = 1 \rightarrow 8 \div 1 = 8$		This is NOT true!
D. $8 \times (3 - 2) = 8 \rightarrow 8 \times 1 = 8$		This is true!

17) Answer: C.

The shape has 6 equal sides. And is side is 4. Then, the perimeter of the shape is:

$4 \times 6 = 24$

18) Answer: C.

$\frac{4}{5} - \frac{3}{5} = \frac{1}{5} = 0.2$

19) Answer: D.

$N = 6$ then: $\frac{36}{6} + 4 = 6 + 4 = 10$

20) Answer: C.

Three people can paint 3 houses in 12 days. It means that for painting 6 houses in 12 days we need 6 people. To paint 6 houses in 6 days, 12 people are needed.

21) Answer: B.

$\frac{18}{27} = \frac{2}{3} = 0.7$, the only choice that is greater than 0.7 is $\frac{5}{2}$.

$\frac{5}{2} = 2.5 , 2.5 > 0.7$

22) Answer: C.

The biggest city is city C and the smallest city is city B.

Number of men in city A is 700 and number of men in city C is 300.

Then: $700 - 300 = 400$

23) Answer: B.

$8.9 - 5.08 = 3.82$, which is closest to 3.8

24) Answer: A.

The value of digit 4 in both numbers x and y are in the tens place. Therefore, they have the same value.

25) Answer: B.

3,489.76853 rounded to the nearest tenth is 3,489.8

26) Answer: A.

$6a + 18 = 48 \rightarrow 6a = 48 - 18$

$6a = 30 \rightarrow a = 5$

27) Answer: D.

All angles in a triangle sum up to 180 degrees.

Two angles of a triangle measure 45 and 65.

$45 + 65 = 110$. Then, the third angle is: $180 - 110 = 70$

28) Answer: C.

$146 + 26 + 10 = 182$

29) Answer: D.

If $\frac{1}{5}$ of a number is greater than 6, the number must be greater than 30.

$\frac{1}{5}x > 6 \rightarrow$ multiply both sides of the inequality by 5, then: $x > 30$

30) Answer: D.

$7 \times (M + N) = 63$, then $M + N = 9$. $M > 0 \rightarrow N \ could \ not \ be \ 9$

31) Answer: C.

The ratio of lions to tigers is 24 to 16 or 3 to 2 at the zoo. Therefore, total number of lions and tigers must be divisible by 5. $3 + 2 = 5$

From the numbers provided, only 76 is not divisible by 5.

32) Answer: C.

A represents digit 6 in the multiplication.

$14 \times 562 = 7,868$

33) Answer: D.

N is even. Let's choose 2 and 4 for N. Now, let's review the choices provided.

A) $\frac{N}{2} = \frac{2}{2} = 1,$ $\frac{N}{2} = \frac{4}{2} = 2,$ One result is odd and the other one is even.

B) $N + 4 = 2 + 4 = 6, 4 + 4 = 8$ Both results are even.

C) $2N = 2 \times 2 = 4, 4 \times 2 = 8$ Both results are even.

D) $N + 1 = 2 + 1 = 3, 4 + 1 = 5$ Both results are odd.

34) Answer: D.

There are equal numbers of four types of cards. Therefore, the total number of cards must be divisible by 4. Only choice D (44) is divisible by 4.

35) Answer: D.

15 seconds is one fourth of a minute. One fourth of 120 is 30.

$120 \div 4 = 30$

Jim types 30 words in 15 seconds.

36) Answer: D.

There are equal

From the choice provided, only choice D is not equal to $\frac{4}{9}$. $\frac{16}{45} = \frac{4}{5}$

37) Answer: C.

The closest to 8.03 is 8 in the choices provided.

38) Answer: c.

Write the numbers in order: 6, 7, 9, 11, 13, 20, 22

Median is the number in the middle. Therefore, the median is 11.

Answers and Explanations

ISEE - Lower Level

Practice Tests 1: Mathematics Achievement

1) Answer: A.

6,563.3752 rounded to the nearest tenth is 6,563.4

2) Answer: C.

One method to compare fractions is to convert them to decimals.

A. $\frac{4}{7} = 0.57$

B. $\frac{1}{5} = 0.2$

C. $\frac{5}{7} = 0.71$

D. $\frac{2}{7} = 0.29$

0.71 or $\frac{5}{7}$ is the largest number.

3) Answer: D.

If 20 balls are removed from the bag at random, there will be one ball in the bag. The probability of choosing a brown ball is 2 out of 20. Therefore, the probability of not choosing a brown ball is 18 out of 20 and the probability of having not a brown ball after removing 18 balls is the same.

4) Answer: B.

The question is this: 2.03 is what percent of 1.45?

Use percent formula: $part = \frac{percent}{100} \times whole$

$part = \frac{percent}{100} \times 1.45 \Rightarrow 2.03 = \frac{percent \times 1.45}{100} \Rightarrow 203 = percent \times 1.45$

$\Rightarrow percent = \frac{203}{1.45} = 140$

5) Answer: D.

The question is this: 423.80 is what percent of 652?

Use percent formula: $part = \frac{percent}{100} \times whole$

$$423.80 = \frac{\text{percent}}{100} \times 652 \Rightarrow 423.80 = \frac{\text{percent} \times 652}{100} \Rightarrow$$

$$64650 = \text{percent} \times 652 \Rightarrow \text{percent} = \frac{42,380}{652} = 65$$

423.80 is 65 % of 652. Therefore, the discount is: $100\% - 65\% = 35\%$

6) Answer: C.

Area of a triangle $= \frac{1}{2}$ (base)(height) $\Rightarrow A = \frac{1}{2}(36)(10) = 180$

7) Answer: A.

All angles in a triangle add up to 180 degrees.

$39 + 45 = 84 \rightarrow 180 - 84 = 96$

8) Answer: D.

Find common denominator and solve.

$$\frac{1}{5} + \frac{3}{4} = \frac{4}{20} + \frac{15}{20} = \frac{19}{20}$$

9) Answer: D.

least common multiple (LCM) of 8 and 15 is the smallest number that is divisible by both 8 and 15. LCM = 120

10) Answer: D.

8 hour = 480 minutes. Write a proportion and solve.

$$\frac{80}{1} = \frac{480}{x} \rightarrow x = \frac{480}{80} = 6$$

11) Answer: A.

Let x be the number of raptors Daniel saw on Monday. Then:

$$Mean = \frac{x+12+15+10+3}{5} = 10 \rightarrow x + 40 \rightarrow x = 50 - 40 = 10$$

12) Answer: C.

The factors of 32 are: {1, 2, 4, 8, 16, 32}

10 is not a factor of 24.

13) Answer: A.

Perimeter $= 2(width + length)$

$A = width \times length$

First, find the length of the rectangle.

Perimeter $= 2(width + length) \rightarrow 84 = 2(11 + length) \rightarrow 168 = 22 + 2(length) \rightarrow 62 = 2(length) \rightarrow length = 31$

$A = 11 \times 31 = 341$

14) Answer: A.

An obtuse angle is an angle of greater than 90 degrees and less than 180 degrees.

Only choice a is an obtuse angle.

15) Answer: D.

There are 10 squares and 6 of them are shaded. Therefore, 6 out of 10 or $\frac{6}{10} = \frac{3}{5}$ are shaded.

16) Answer: B.

Write a proportion and solve. $\frac{2}{3} = \frac{x}{60}$

Use cross multiplication: $3x = 120 \rightarrow x = 40$

17) Answer: D.

To find the discount, multiply the number by (100% – rate of discount).

Therefore, for the first discount we get: $(300)(100\% - 35\%) = (300)(0.65)$

For the next 25 % discount: $(300)(0.65)(0.75)$

18) Answer: D.

A quadrilateral with one pair of parallel sides is a trapezoid.

19) Answer: A.

Plug in 40 for A in the equation. Only choice A works.

$A + 40 = 80 \rightarrow 40 + 40 = 80$

20) Answer: C.

$1 \ hour: \$2.25. \ 8 \ hours: 8 \times \$2.25 = \$18$

21) Answer: A.

There are 72 students in the class. 30 of the are male and 42 of them are female.

42 out of 72 are female. Then:

$\frac{42}{72} = \frac{x}{100} \rightarrow 4,200 = 72x \rightarrow x = 4,200 \div 72 \approx 58\%$

22) Answer: B.

1 pizza has 8 slices. 16 pizzas contain (16 × 8) 128 slices.

23) Answer: D.

Since Mike running at 5.5 miles per hour and Julia is running at the speed of 6 miles per hour, each hour their distance decreases by 0.5 mile. So, it takes 19 hours to cover distance of 9.5 miles. 8.5 ÷ 0.5 = 19

24) Answer: C.

$0.045 \times 100 = 4.5\%$

25) Answer: B.

Since Julie gives 3 pieces of candy to each of her friends, then, then number of pieces of candies must be divisible by 3.

A. $97 \div 3 = 32.333$

B. $156 \div 3 = 52$

C. $356 \div 3 = 118.666$

D. $223 \div 3 = 74.333$

Only choice B gives a whole number.

26) Answer: A.

$\$6 \times 10 = \$60$

Petrol use: $10 \times 4 = 40$ liters

Petrol cost: $40 \times \$1 = \$40$

Money earned: $\$60 - \$40 = \$20$

27) Answer: B.

$\frac{4}{100} = 0.04$

28) Answer: C.

$$
\begin{array}{r}
35 \text{ hr. } 10 \text{ min.} \\
- 23 \text{ hr. } 38 \text{ min.} \\
\hline
11 \text{hr. } 32 \text{min.}
\end{array}
$$

29) Answer: D.

The failing rate is 30 out of $180 = \frac{30}{180}$

Change the fraction to percent: $\frac{30}{180} \times 100\% = 17\%$

17 percent of students failed. Therefore, 63 percent of students passed the exam.

30) Answer: D.

If the length of the box is 18, then the width of the box is one third of it, 9, and the height of the box is 3 (one third of the width). The volume of the box is:

V=(length)(width)(height) $= (18)(9)(3) = 486$ cm^3

Answers and Explanations

ISEE - Lower Level

Practice Tests 2: Quantitative Reasoning

1) Answer: B.

$$6 + 3 = 9, \quad 9 + 4 = 13, \quad 13 + 5 = 18, \quad 18 + 6 = 24$$

2) Answer: C.

The length of the rectangle is 12. Then, its width is 3.

$$12 \div 4 = 3$$

Perimeter of a rectangle $= 2 \times width + 2 \times length = 2 \times 3 + 2 \times 12 = 6 + 24 = 30$

3) Answer: C.

$Mary's\ Money = y;\ John's\ Money = y + 10$

$John\ gives\ Mary\ \$16 \rightarrow y + 10 - 16 = y - 6$

4) Answer: D.

Dividing 106 by 8 leaves a remainder of 2.

5) Answer: C.

$7,000 + A - 400 = 8,700 \rightarrow 7,000 + A = 8,700 + 400$

$\rightarrow A = 9,100 - 7,000 = 2,100$

6) Answer: D.

79 divided by 6, the remainder is 1. 37 divided by 6, the remainder is also 1.

7) Answer: A.

$105 off is the same as 35 percent off. Thus, 35 percent of a number is 105.

Then: $35\% \ of\ x = 105 \rightarrow 0.35x = 105 \rightarrow x = \frac{105}{0.35} = 300$

8) Answer: A.

$\frac{5}{2} = 2.5$, the only choice provided that is less than 2.5 is choice A.

$\frac{5}{2} = 2.5 > 1.7$

9) Answer: D.

$x + 3 = 7 \rightarrow x = 4$

$6y = 36 \rightarrow y = 6$

$y - x = 6 - 4 = 2$

10) Answer: C.

$362 - x + 112 = 280 \rightarrow 474 - x = 280 \rightarrow 474 = 280 + x$

$\rightarrow x = 474 - 280 = 194$

11) Answer: C.

All angles in a triangle sum up to 180 degrees. The triangle provided is an isosceles triangle. In an isosceles triangle, the three angles are 45, 45, and 90 degrees. Therefore, the value of x is 45.

12) Answer: D.

15 percent of $33.00 is $18. (Remember that 15 percent is equal to one fourth)

13) Answer: C.

$11.08 - 6.6 = 4.48$

14) Answer: A.

$\frac{5}{2} - \frac{3}{2} = \frac{2}{2} = 1$

15) Answer: C.

TWO times a number N is $2 \times N$. When 3 is added to it, the result is: $5 + (2 \times N) = 25 \rightarrow 2N + 5 = 25$

16) Answer: B.

$48 = 2 \times N + 16 \rightarrow 2N = 46 - 14 = 32 \rightarrow N = 16$

17) Answer: A.

$3,400 - 625 = 2,775$

18) Answer: B.

4 percent of $650 = \frac{4}{100} \times 650 = \frac{1}{25} \times 650 = \frac{650}{25} = 26$

19) Answer: D.

$32 \div (3 + 5) = 32 \div 8 = 4$ not 5

20) Answer: D.

$$\text{Speed} = \frac{distance}{time}$$

$$68 = \frac{2,600}{time} \rightarrow time = \frac{2,600}{68} = 38.24$$

It takes Nicole about 38 hours to go from city A to city B.

21) Answer: C.

$$\frac{12}{25} = 0.48$$

22) Answer: D.

9 is NOT a prime factor.

23) Answer: B.

$$140 \div 20 = 7$$

24) Answer: B.

Let's order number of pants sold per month:

$$65, 70, 85, 88, 90, 110$$

Median is the number in the middle. Since, there are 6 numbers (an even number) the Median is the average of numbers 3 and 4: Median is: $\frac{85+88}{2} = 86.5$

25) Answer: B.

$$350 + 35 = 385$$

26) Answer: A.

$$14a + 20 = 160$$

$$14a = 160 - 20$$

$$14a = 140 \Rightarrow a = 10$$

27) Answer: B.

Thousandths

28) Answer: C.

$$\frac{55}{1,000} = 0.055$$

29) Answer: C.

$\frac{1}{3}$ of 21 hours is 6 hours. $\frac{1}{3} \times 21 = \frac{21}{3} = 7$

30) Answer: C.

The ratio of red marbles to blue marbles is 6 to 2. Therefore, the total number of marbles must be divisible by 8.

$6 + 2 = 8$

55 is the only one that is not divisible by 8.

31) Answer: B.

Area of a square $= side \times side = 81 \rightarrow side = 9$

Perimeter of a square $= 4 \times side = 4 \times 9 = 36$

32) Answer: D.

$300 + \square - 180 = 1,200 \rightarrow 120 + \square = 1,200$

$\square = 1,200 - 120 = 1,080$

33) Answer: C.

$\frac{1}{4}$ of students are girls. Therefore, $\frac{3}{4}$ of students in the class are boys. $\frac{3}{4}$ of 80 is 60.

There are 60 boys in the class. $\frac{3}{4} \times 60 = \frac{180}{4} = 45$

34) Answer: A.

$N \times (7 - 5) = 32 \rightarrow N \times 2 = 32 \rightarrow N = 16$

35) Answer: B.

If $x \blacksquare y = 4x + y - 5$, Then:

$2 \blacksquare 10 = 4(2) + 10 - 5 = 8 + 10 - 5 = 13$

36) Answer: C.

Of the numbers provided, 0.5923 is the greatest.

37) Answer: A.

$\frac{7}{8} - \frac{3}{4} = \frac{7}{8} - \frac{6}{8} = \frac{1}{8} = 0.125$

38) Answer: B.

The closest number to 3.03 is 3.

Answers and Explanations

ISEE - Lower Level

Practice Tests 2: Mathematics Achievement

1) Answer: C.

The factors of 16 are: $\{1, 2, 4, 8, 16\}$

The factors of 32 are: $\{1, 2, 4, 8, 16, 32\}$

greatest common factor (GCF) = 16

2) Answer: A.

Sixty-two thousand, five hundred nineteen is written as 62,519.

3) Answer: D.

The name of a rectangle with sides of equal length is square.

4) Answer: C.

The question is that number 36,573.13 is how many times of number 3.657313.

The answer is 10,000.

5) Answer: B.

Use the Pythagorean Theorem to find the length of the third side:

$a^2 + b^2 = c^2 \Longrightarrow 6^2 + 8^2 = c^2$

$100 = c^2 \Longrightarrow c = 10$

The perimeter of the triangle is: $6 + 8 + 10 = 24$

6) Answer: A.

Simplify each choice provided using order of operations rules.

A. $5 - (-2) + (-27) = 5 + 2 - 27 = -20$

B. $-5 + (-5) \times (-4) = -5 + 20 = 15$

C. $-6 \times (-4) + (-2) \times (-7) = 24 + 14 = 38$

D. $(-2) \times (-15) + 20 = 30 + 20 = 50$

Only choice A is -20.

7) Answer: C.

Lily eats 24 pancakes in 1 minute ⇒ Lily eats 4×3 pancakes in 3 minutes.

Ella eats 2 ½ pancakes in 1 minute ⇒ Ella eats $2 \, ½ \times 3$ pancakes in 3 minutes.

In total Lily and Ella eat $12 + 7.5 = 19.5$ pancakes in 5 minutes.

8) Answer: C.

$0.82 + 1.5 + 3.23 = 5.55$

9) Answer: B.

Perimeter of a rectangle $= 2(length + width) = 2(8 + 5) = 26$

10) Answer: D.

To solve this problem, divide $6\frac{1}{3}$ by $\frac{1}{9}$.

$6\frac{1}{3} \div \frac{1}{9} = \frac{19}{3} \div \frac{1}{9} = \frac{19}{3} \times \frac{9}{1} = 57$

11) Answer: B.

$\frac{7}{11}$ means 7 is divided by 11. The fraction line simply means division or $\div$.

Therefore, we can write $\frac{7}{11}$ as $7 \div 11$.

12) Answer: C.

Subtract hours: $2 - 5 = - 3$

Subtract the minutes: $15 - 30 = - 15$

The minutes are less than 0, so:

Add 60 to minutes ($-15 + 60 = 45$ minutes)

Subtract 1 from hours ($-3 - 1 = -4$) the hours are less than 0, add 12: ($12 - 4 = 8$)

The answer is 20:45 that is equal to 8:45

13) Answer: A.

From choices provided, only 14 is NOT a multiple of 6.

14) Answer: C.

Area $= width \times height$

Area $= 84$, $Width = 4$. $\Rightarrow 84 = 4 \times height$

height $= \frac{84}{4} = 21$

15) Answer: B.

Low temperature is 44°f cooler than the temperature at 12:00 PM that is 66°f, that means low temperature is 32°f (76°f − 44°f).

16) Answer: B.

$(8^2 − 4^2) \div (4^2 \div 2) = (64 − 16) \div (16 \div 2) = (48) \div (8) = 6$

17) Answer: C.

$27,760 \leq 28,069 \leq 29,521 \leq 29,562$

18) Answer: C.

$3.23 + 13.65 + 2.50 + 4.66 + 10.34 =$

$3 + 14 + 3 + 5 + 10 = 35$

19) Answer: B.

The line is from 5 to −2. $5 − (− 2) = 5 + 2 = 7$

20) Answer: D.

Find the least common denominator (LCD), then rewriting each term as an equivalent fraction with the LCD. Then we compare the numerators of each fraction and put them in correct order from least to greatest or greatest to least.

LCD of 2, 8, 4 and 16 is 16. Rewrite the input fractions as equivalent fractions using the LCD:

A. $\frac{24}{16}$ B. $\frac{8}{16}$ C. $\frac{20}{16}$ B. $\frac{7}{16}$

So, Answer: D has the least value.

21) Answer: C.

The first picture is divided to 12 parts that 3 parts of it is shaded ($\frac{3}{12} = \frac{1}{4}$). The second picture is divided to 8 parts that 3 parts of that is shaded ($\frac{3}{8}$).

22) Answer: C.

The digit 6 has a value of $6 \times \frac{1}{100}$

The digit 7 has a value of 7×1000

The digit 5 has a value of $5 \times 10 = 50$

The digit 1 has a value of $1 \times \dfrac{1}{10}$

23) Answer: B.

Three – digit odd numbers that have a 6 in the hundreds place and a 3 in the tens place are 631, 633, 635, 637, 639. 637 is one of the choices.

24) Answer: C.

0.58 is equal to $\dfrac{58}{100} = \dfrac{29}{25}$

25) Answer: B.

average (mean) $= \dfrac{sum\ of\ terms}{number\ of\ terms} = \dfrac{4+10+13+16+19+16+14.4}{7} = 13.2$

26) Answer: A.

probability $= \dfrac{desired\ outcomes}{possible\ outcomes} = \dfrac{5}{5+6+8+10} = \dfrac{5}{29}$

27) Answer: A.

To find total number of students in Riddle Elementary school, add number of all students.

$65 + 16 = 81$

28) Answer: D.

$1\ year = 365\ days, 1\ day = 24\ hours$

$1\ year = 365 \times 24$

$1\ year = 8,760$

29) Answer: A.

$\dfrac{17}{21} \cong 0.81$

30) Answer: D.

$30 \times 12 = 360$

"End"

Made in the USA
Coppell, TX
13 March 2020